D1104559

LOVE THEM AND LEAD THEM

HOW TO UNLEASH THE SUPER POWER OF RELATIONSHIPS TO MAKE YOU A HIGHLY EFFECTIVE AND INFLUENTIAL LEADER!

JEROME LOVE

Published by GUGOGS™ Leadership Institute
Copyright © 2013 by Jerome Love.
All rights reserved.

Love Them and Lead Them
How to Unleash the Super Power of Relationships to Make You a Highly
Effective and Influential Leader!

ISBN: 978-0-9851074-1-3

Please send your comments to the address below.
Thank you in advance.

GUGOGS™ Leadership Institute
Jerome Love
www.jeromelove.com
12401 S. Post Oak, Suite 218, Houston, TX 77045

This book is available at quantity discounts for bulk purchases.
To order, visit www.jeromelove.com

.

Printed in the United States of America.

ACKNOWLEDGEMENTS

I'd like to first thank my wife Stevenia, who was one of the first people to look past many of my relational deficiencies and love me in spite of them. Then to my four children, Jasmyn, Jayda, Jaleya, and Jerome, who inspire me and who have taught me firsthand and through observation many of the principles of this book about innate human behaviors.

To the brothers of the Epsilon Iota Chapter of Alpha Phi Alpha Fraternity, from whom I learned a great deal about leadership, I'd like to say thank you.

To my LB's, I love you guys like brothers; Tim Johnson and Aaron Terry, I appreciate all you do, and without you I seriously doubt I'd be the man I am today; Alejandro Vasquez, who helped me start my first business by printing my T-Shirts for free, and told me in 1999, "Jerome, you are going to be a huge success, but you have to learn how to deal with people." You were the first person that made me really evaluate my interpersonal skills.

Derrick Love, without you and, of course, your creation of GUGOGS™ I am honestly clueless as to where I would be today. Then to the other Derrick, Derrick Reed, you have been with me from GUGOGS™, to LHS Realty Group, and now Texas Black Expo; you are a tremendous friend. Houston City Council Member Larry Green, thanks for being a tremendous model of leadership. My mentors Jonathan Sprinkles and

Revis Laws, I appreciate you guys for all you have shared with me and taught me, from marketing to investing, much of my financial success is a result of your wisdom.

To my parents John and Calner Love, thanks for laying a proper foundation, for without it I would not have been about to grow.

Then last but not least, to my pastor, Dr. Dana Carson, everything I know about leadership, from understanding personalities, to communication skills, to verbal and non-verbal communication, I learned from you. You are a tremendous leader and an awesome model.

CONTENTS

READ THIS FIRST

What I'm about to share with you will likely shock you.

Most people who call themselves leaders don't have a clue about how to effectively lead! You're probably thinking, "That doesn't make any sense. If they're in a leadership position, obviously they're leaders." Right? Wrong!

If you're among the millions of folks who think leadership is about a tag or a title, you're in for a rude awakening. In fact, unless you change your approach and perspective on leadership, you'll likely be doomed to a cycle of frustration and stagnation within your family, team, company, or organization.

You see, leadership has nothing to do with your degrees, previous accomplishments, and all the other faulty information traditional leadership books teach. Most of those books teach you to focus on sharpening *your* tools rather than recognizing the power within the individuals and teams following you.

While most business leadership seminars and books would have you draft *your* personal vision, discuss *your* goals, *your* strengths, and other self-centered leadership activities that often leave you unequipped to be an effective and influential leader, very few, if any, reveal the real truth about effective leadership. Leadership is not about *you*!

Now, clearly, there are qualities and skills that must be developed before people will listen to or follow you, but that's only 40 percent of the battle. The other 60 percent of your efforts should be directed toward the wants, needs, and desires of those under your leadership.

At the core of *Love Them and Lead Them* is a bold new approach to leadership at any level. Whether the organization is a Fortune 500 company, a collegiate student organization, a church, or a family of four, the Love Them and Lead Them leadership model will help you fulfill your organization's goals and get you closer to your potential.

You see, most leaders only look the part of a leader. They're often outgoing, educated, and articulate, but most of them are also like shiny new cars without fuel. They're not going anywhere. People provide the fuel for great leadership. No followers, no leadership.

My leadership model is simple, yet deadly effective. It wasn't developed in a classroom by listening to so-called leadership scholars, nor is it the result of solely reading the latest books written by today's leadership icons. My methods come from 17 years of quasi-leadership experience in business and social organizations where I failed miserably.

My leadership curriculum, if you will, is also the result of losing thousands of dollars in failed business ventures and absolutely obliterating a number of relationships because I relied more on the "title" of leadership rather than developing my abysmal relationship-building skills.

These failed businesses and relational struggles, which I'll happily discuss further in the book, for the most part share one commonality: I was unable to influence my team in some cases, and potential business partners in other instances. As a matter of fact in many cases, not only was I unable to influence them, I also completely alienated them to the point that they thought I was a total jerk. Guess what happened most of the time in those situations? I wouldn't get the deal, or worse, I'd be demonized for my insensitive behavior when I thought I was simply displaying good ol' aggressive leadership.

You've already figured it out. When it came to leadership, I was clueless. Blithely unaware of one fundamental leadership truth: **You have ZERO influence if people don't like you**. That's your first lesson. There'll be plenty more before we're done, so buckle up.

WHO SHOULD READ THIS BOOK?

Love Them and Lead Them contains leadership jewels for anyone aspiring to lead or currently leading, but because I'm an entrepreneur and CEO, of course I'm writing from that perspective. However, the principles are also extremely relevant and applicable for pastors, parents, trainers, educators, teachers, salespeople, job seekers, and even employees. *Love Them and Lead Them* is about developing high level communication skills, better relationships, and magnetic influence.

If you desire to improve in any or all of those three areas at home, play, or work, this book's for you. Even if you don't consider yourself a leader, you'll enjoy this book. I write the way I teach and train in my leadership seminars. I'm a high energy, down-to-earth kinda guy who likes to throw in stories to illustrate concepts because I know how much we all love to read a good story. In fact, my friend Reshonda Tate Billingsley, a best-selling author of 30-plus fiction books and a masterful storyteller in her own right, told me after reading my first book, "I normally don't even read nonfiction, but I loved your book."

Rest assured, you've made a smart investment, and I promise you'll certainly enjoy the ride.

WHAT'S THE BOTTOM LINE?

If you're like me, sometimes you like to skip the small talk and get straight to the point. So for those folks, here's the bottom line of the book. The key to successful leadership lies in your ability to understand, communicate with, and influence people.

I'll focus heavily on relationship building because I believe relationships are the foundation of any successful leader. Leaders rise and fall based upon the team they have around them. That team must feel you value and respect them. And *you* must understand their wants, fears, needs, and desires. As a leader you're also in the brand-development business. Your goal is to create a brand that says, I'm a likeable, respectable, honest person, and I'm someone you need to follow. So we'll spend some time discussing your leadership brand as well.

HOW'S THE BOOK ORGANIZED?

This book is broken down into three sections. Section One is about the Psychology of Leadership. Section Two is all about Conflict Resolution. Section Three is about Influence.

In Section One we'll start to unlock the hidden secrets essential to influence—understanding why people behave the way they do and what drives them to follow certain leaders. You'll learn about four primary personality types and how to quickly identify these personality types on your team.

You'll also learn how to place these people in positions where they will naturally prosper and help the organization achieve its goals. In addition, once you identify them, I'll give you the keys to flipping automatic switches that will make them more likely to respond favorably to your leadership. Sprinkled throughout are Love's Laws of Leadership, which are some of my closely guarded tips I've never shared with anyone outside my private seminars. You'll dig those too.

In Section Two, we get into conflict. If you can change your approach to resolving conflict, you'll be on your way to magnificent leadership. So often conflict's perceived as negative or bad, but that's only because leaders haven't been equipped to make conflict work in their organizations. This is where relationship building becomes so important.

All of us have a need for social affirmation. So before you barge into an employee's office to gruffly ask, "Where's that report?" which will likely cause a bit of anxiety and conflict, you need to first engage in social conversation.

Ask them how their weekend was, how the wife and kids are, how was vacation? Then take care of the business at hand. This is a part of my 3-Step Connection Plan that you're gonna love.

Leadership is easy when everyone thinks the same way, has the same goals, and has the same vision. But what happens when you have a person on your team that has a different opinion? Do you just say, "I'm in charge, so do what I say"? Do you fire them, assuming they're a detriment to the team because they don't agree with everything you say? Or do you embrace diversity? We'll talk about that in Section Two.

Diversity isn't good just in relationships; in companies, it's *essential*. Without diversity there would never be any new ideas, and innovation would be stifled. In this section, I'm going to show you why conflict is never bad, but that there can be ineffective approaches to dealing with conflict that result in negative consequences.

At the core, conflict is nothing more than difference: a difference of opinion, a difference in approach, and/or a difference in communication. You thought one thing and someone else thought another. So I'll give you techniques I know will help you become a better communicator. Additionally, I'll share with you what I have coined as my S.T.O.P. Analysis. "S.T.O.P." is an acronym that stands for Significance, Timing, Outcome, and Pattern. This is the litmus test any good leader must pass in order to determine whether or not to address an issue or not in that moment.

Sometimes effective conflict resolution has more to do with timing than content. In other words, you'll learn how addressing conflict at the wrong time can be just as detrimental as not addressing it at all.

One of my favorite—and most deadly effective—techniques is what I call the Law of Permission. This law simply states a person cannot get offended if you ask for their permission. For instance, let's say you have an employee who's exhibited behavior detrimental to the team, and you want to assign them a mentor. You could go to them and say, "Your behavior has been completely unacceptable. I'm going to assign you a mentor so this doesn't happen again," or you could say, "I really want you to be a success here, but I'm concerned about your behavior. In order to ensure you meet your goals, I'd like to assign you a mentor. Is that okay with you?" Which of these approaches do you think would be received more positively? Number two obviously. But why? You said the same thing, but in the second scenario you didn't tell them what you were going to do; you simply asked for their permission.

Who can get offended when you ask for their permission to help them? The key words are, "Is that okay with you?" Five small words that can have a huge effect on minimizing offense when dealing with conflict. The first scenario violates the Law of Attack, which states if a person is attacked, they will defend themselves. And when people are defensive, productivity comes to a screeching halt.

The third and final section is about influence.

As I shared earlier, influence is the cornerstone of exceptional leadership. A leader must have followers that are willing to follow. If you attempt to force them to follow, it's called slavery and it will ultimately lead to a revolt. However, if you're able to grow your influence effectively, both you and your followers are fulfilled. Influence is all around us. Even before we were born, we were influencing.

A hungry baby who wants to be fed does what? They may cry. They may scream. They're attempting to influence you to change their diaper or get them a bottle. When you're in high school, you may want to take a certain guy or girl to the prom. This requires influence. You interview for a job and there are six other candidates. How do you influence the company to choose you? We'll examine several different scenarios.

In this section I'll share five keys to successful influence that, when utilized properly, will propel your leadership quotient to an extraordinary level.

MY PLEDGE TO YOU!

If you desire to be a more influential and effective leader, you're in the right place, reading the right book, with the right coach.

Love Them and Lead Them will shed light on and unlock the true keys to effective leadership: high functioning, communication-based relationships! It's a comprehensive blueprint for building and maintaining high levels of influence.

Leaders are the guiding lights in every organization, in every family, and on every team. A unit will rise and fall based on the strength of its leadership. That's an awesome responsibility. But it's also a tremendous honor. I have no doubt you can do it. You wouldn't have invested in this book if you didn't *want* to do it.

You're halfway there. Love Them and Lead Them focuses on four core principles: creating a magnetic brand, understanding the psychology of amazing leaders, and communicating and connecting in a way that others will respect and respond to so that you will have phenomenal influence.

You've shown me you have the courage to take the reins of your own personal development. *Love Them and Lead Them* will now take you from where you are today to where you want to be tomorrow. No gimmicks. No games. No hype. Just straight talk on how to develop magnetic relationships, become a super influential leader who consistently yields exponential—and yes—immediate results!

Ready to go? Let do this!

Jerome Love

Introduction:
The Love Them and Lead Them Story

It was the spring of 2009 and things just weren't adding up. I was running three companies in three hot industries, but nothing was going the way I'd planned. Nothing.

As I took in the humidity in my hometown of Houston, driving about 15 miles per hour along Loop 610 and looking at the incredible skyline, I couldn't help wondering why certain parts of my life were so jacked up.

By now I should've been a gazillionaire with yachts and homes in the Hamptons, I thought to myself. Okay, maybe not the Hamptons thing but you get my point. I felt I should've been farther along than I was at that point in my life.

So, as I bobbed and weaved out of the notorious Houston rush-hour traffic, I just screamed, "That's it! I'm done! I can't do this anymore!" You see, in my mind I'd done everything imaginable to make it all work, so why wasn't it working?

I had the right business cards, owned the right suits, and belonged to the right networking groups. Why then, didn't I have the right kind of *success?* What was I missing? I'd read all the right books. Attended all the right conferences and prayed all the right prayers. Was someone playing some elaborate prank on me? Surely I deserved better than this. What was I missing?

Had I been duped into buying into the American dream? I didn't get it. Why did it look like I was successful on the outside while I was dying on the inside?

It simply wasn't adding up! You see, I had three primary businesses, and all of them had million-dollar potential.

The first one, the Texas Black Expo, was a trade-show marketing company I founded in 2004. The premise was to provide a gathering place for people of African descent to come and mingle with companies that were interested in black consumers. Houston is a mecca of black folks with companies clamoring to get in front of this desirable demographic.

Great idea, right? Yeah, that's what I thought too until I found myself $100,000 in the hole after Year 1. Like most start-up entrepreneurs I was running that business by the hair on my chinny chin-chin and flying by the seat of my pants.

Fortunately, by Year 3 we (and by "we," I mean mostly "I") had dug out of that hole and by Year 5 we'd quadrupled our sponsor sales from 2004 and were now seeing substantial profits. As the notorious bad boy Charlie Sheen would say, "I was winning." Or so I thought.

That's when it happened.

The economy collapsed. Washington Mutual, who was our primary bank sponsor, collapsed. General Motors, which was "the Official Car of the Texas Black Expo," was on the brink of collapse. Suddenly, we were scrounging to catch our breath. Those two heavy hitters alone, coupled with a few other sponsors, represented more than 60 percent of our sponsor revenue and suddenly they'd all vanished? In less than a second we went from thriving to barely surviving. We went from becoming the potential million-dollar baby to another casualty of a bad economy.

But wait, there's more.

In 2007, while gasping for air with the Black Expo, I started Jerome Love Enterprises, a professional development corporation, to house my speaking, consulting, and publishing ventures.

My other love was personal development. I'd started doing motivational speaking and leadership training and development presentations around the Houston area as well as nationally, and I was enjoying my newfound freedom as a solopreneur.

I was starting to build my brand as a young entrepreneur, and I was getting invited to speak at a number of conferences such as the Collegiate Entrepreneurs Organizations National Conference and the National Alliance of Black School Educators Conference, just to name a couple. Sounds exciting, right? Unfortunately, if you know anything about the realities of launching a new speaking business, you also know the bookings weren't consistent enough to pay the bills.

But wait, there's more.

Around the same time that I started the Black Expo (circa 2004), I also launched a third company, LHS Realty Group, a full-service real estate company based in Missouri City, Texas, a thriving metropolis right outside Houston.

I launched the company in 2004 and by 2006 had grown it to a team of seven agents. Real estate's always fascinated me, and with my flair for talking to people, coupled with my relentless hustle, I knew I'd be able to do well. And I did. At least for a while. I'm an avid reader, and I'd learned from big real estate moguls to train my agents to be great at selling. But from time to time, I would personally get involved in the process of listing or selling a home myself. However, my primary goal was to train my agents to generate the sales like the real estate big dogs!

As the real estate company grew, the time I spent with the other two businesses became pretty limited. I was pretty much neglecting them because I was getting such a great return with the real estate. Besides, I believed that training my agents would mean a huge payday soon, so I kept my eyes on the real estate prize.

For about 18 months, things were going as planned. We were listing houses left and right, and I was right where I thought I should be for a new real estate empire.

Then the unthinkable—yet hardly surprising—thing happened. The economy tanked. To make matters worse, my top agent joined the police force, another one decided to pursue his dream of becoming a barber, another three called it quits altogether, another moved to a new city, and the last one decided to leave and go work for a cross-town competitor!

What else could go wrong? I hadn't prepared for this level of catastrophe because honestly, I didn't believe it could happen to me. Maybe that's why I'd become a serial entrepreneur, so that I'd always have a "Plan B" if my "Plan A" didn't work. Yet things were not adding up for me financially, and I was starting to question every business decision I'd ever made. How could I have been so off the mark?

That night when I arrived home, I sat in the driveway for about an hour. I wasn't ready to face my other responsibilities yet. I needed answers.

As I sat there staring into nowhere, I was forced to come to terms with the fact that there was a disconnect between the way people perceived me and my actual reality. Some of you know what I'm talking about. As the President of the Texas Black Expo, I'm a very visible figure within the Houston community. An outsider looking at this event, which broke attendance records each year, would have thought the brand had become a mega hit. And in some ways it had.

I was proud of the fact that I'd created something from nothing and turned it into an annual event people loved. I felt a great sense of accomplishment that I'd simply taken an idea and created a budding empire that could possibly be duplicated in other cities.

But then there were also the realities of running a success-ful enterprise. So, when I was alone with the Expo's books and facing the numbers, I didn't feel like such a success. Had I contributed to this warped perception of me?

Add to my Expo celebrity the fact that I'm an outgoing author and motivational speaker who makes part of his living teaching people how to have successful lives and businesses. Most people thought I was rolling in the dough but I wasn't. It's tough when people perceive you a certain way and have expectations based upon that perception, but yet you're un-able to live up to the hype. The reality of that statement led me to declare, "I'm done!" For the first time in my life, I began to question if I was cut out to be a businessman. That was one of the lowest days of my life, but it was hardly the last low day I would have, unfortunately.

THE MAN IN THE MIRROR

There are generally two kinds of people in the world. Those who, when things go wrong, tend to blame others and those who blame themselves. My tendency is to blame myself. So, there I was, a self-pitying, struggling pseudo entrepreneur with no clue about how I was going to escape the deep hole I'd dug for myself and the dark cave I'd crawled into.

I had to face some hard facts: All of my businesses were on life support and the only common denominator was—me. The pain of that reality plunged me into momentary insanity. I could hardly stand to accept I had screwed up my life that bad, so I created a new reality for me to escape the pain. I wasn't ready to admit I was a screw-up just yet.

I had the answer: *I'll get an MBA.* That'll fix everything, I told myself. Isn't that what the world tries to make us believe? That if we just get the right education all our troubles will be over? Well, that's partly correct. I did need an education. But it wasn't the kind of schooling you get from sitting in a hard chair at the local university.

I was sold on my MBA idea, but I thought I'd run it by my mentor, Jonathan Sprinkles, just for good measure. Jonathan is a successful coach and speaker who's made millions. I'd learned a lot about growing my business from watching him build his. "Jon, I'm thinking about getting my MBA, man," I said to him over lunch one day. "Whadaya think?"

Be careful asking that question. Jonathan finished chewing his food and squinted his eyes as he thought about my question. "An MBA, huh?" he said.

"Yeah, I mean, that's gotta be the answer. I can get an executive one on the weekends and—"

"You don't need an MBA, man."

"I don't?" I said, shocked and curious at the same time.

"No," he said leaning forward. "I gotta get to a meeting right now, but meet me Wednesday at Starbucks on Westheimer. I wanna give you something. It's exactly what you need."

"What is it?" I asked, even more perplexed.

"Just meet me Wednesday."

A few days later I caught up with Jonathan and he handed me a booklet. "What's this?" I asked, looking at the small leaflet-looking materials.

"It's what you need. You asked me what I thought. And this is what I think. This is what you need," he chuckled. "Read it."

And just like that, he was gone.

I sat in the always loud Starbucks, staring at the leaflet and then out the window as I watched Jon drive away. "What in the hell?"

Now, I don't know about you, but when I ask for advice, I don't expect people to give me a booklet written by someone I've never heard of. But that's exactly what Jonathan did.

As I watched him pull out of the parking lot, I looked down at the booklet. Dan Kennedy. *Who in the heck is Dan Kennedy?*

That night after I'd put my kids to bed, I flipped through the Kennedy book, wondering why my mentor thought this was the answer to all my anguish. It looked interesting, but I was too tired to start reading it, so I tossed it on the table, headed to the shower, and went to bed. Dan Kennedy would have to wait.

The next morning, Jonathan texted me. "You finish the book yet?"

I wanted to say "yes," like the good student, but I was honest. "Naw, man, haven't gotten around to it yet. But I will."

His response was classic. "Read it."

A few days later I finally got around to Kennedy's booklet. I was still kinda miffed that Jon hadn't offered me any other words of wisdom. After all, I thought that's what coaches and mentors did. Instead, mine had given me a booklet? Thanks a lot, Jon.

Now, some of you will feel me on this next piece. When you have kids, sometimes your time is never your own. That day I was trying to squeeze in some "me" time while my kids were preoccupied.

I had a few choices. I could play golf or I could read the "booklet." It had been a while since I'd hit the links, and the day was unusually clear and the humidity unusually low for Houston. My decision was easy. I was playing golf. So I looked through my phone to call and get a tee time, and of course, as fate would have it, I stumbled upon Jonathan's last text: "Read it." I tried to ignore it but I couldn't.

"Damn," I thought. "I told Jon I'd read this book." So I hung up the phone, took a seat on the side of my bed, and started reading. Right off the bat I knew Jonathan was right.

This book was exactly what I needed. Dan Kennedy, for those unfamiliar with his feats, is a marketing genius. He does a lot of training and consulting for small businesses and specializes in direct mail marketing. His ultimate premise and foundation for most of his teaching is that most businesses fail because they don't market at all or they don't do it right.

Nothing earth-shattering, I thought as I read the first few pages. I know *this stuff*. Yet I kept reading. Kennedy asks some interesting questions. What do most people do when they start a business? They go to the equivalent of their library—the bookstore or the Internet. We buy books and study billion-dollar corporations such as McDonald's, Apple, Ford or General Electric. And while there are lots of things we can learn from these corporations, we have to understand that, in many regards, their realities are light-years apart from ours as small business owners.

Nike can afford to spend $1 million on a Super Bowl ad featuring only a swoosh sign and the words "Just Do it"; we can't. Apple can buy a billboard in the middle of Times Square with just a black backdrop and a white apple in the center of it, and everyone knows exactly whose brand that is. That's not most entrepreneurs' reality. And it certainly wasn't mine!

After I'd shed my "I know everything" cape, I started to see why Kennedy was so revered in the marketing space. His philosophy is that as a small business owner, you can't afford to spend all your money "branding" your business, but that doesn't mean you don't spend effort figuring out your brand by being smarter and by creating sales! Whoa. That was the first ton of bricks that hit me. I'd definitely tried to do steak branding on a ground-beef budget. Anybody else know what I'm talking about?

Your number one goal is to get your phone to ring. To get people calling you about your business. To increase your leads.

So instead of treating your advertising as an expanded business card, instead of assuming that if people knew you existed they'd choose to do business with you, Kennedy suggested entrepreneurs do everything in their power to create value for customers around their products and services.

His focus is on creating value that distinguishes your business from the alternatives, which is predicated upon first understanding the **customer**. Marketing—not networking—is the key to a hugely successful business. However, the key is it has to be strategic, targeted marketing based upon those you desire to attract. Magnetic marketing.

Now I know you're probably thinking, "I thought this was a book about leadership, not marketing," but stick with me here and I'll bring it all home. Kennedy's booklet got me thinking about a critical step in becoming a leader: creating a magnetic leadership **brand.**

Successful brands are successful at getting people to follow them for one reason: They understand their core audience. Ever been in a conversation with a coworker or friend and they said, "You're not listening to me" or "You don't understand"? Ever notice the sheer anguish on their faces when they said those things?

Now, take a picture in time of another conversation when you said to the same individual, "Oh, yes! Now I understand!" Did you notice the change in their physiology and body language? It was probably night and day.

That's my point here. Most leaders can't lead because they haven't committed to understanding what their followers need or want. You're reading this book right now because you believe what? That you'll gain additional insights on leadership, right?

Likewise, people will follow you for only one reason: They believe you're going to get them closer to their own desires, wants, needs, and goals. They do not follow for any other reason. Never forget that.

THE BUSIEST DRIVE-THROUGH ON EARTH

People have studied the success of McDonald's for decades, but few people realize that the question of hamburger superiority can be answered only by the consumer. Some might argue that because McDonald's sells more franchises than other burger joints, they have better burgers. Not necessarily. What sales represent that's germane to our discussion on leadership branding is this: McDonald's understands its customers better than other hamburger operators.

Here's why.

If you'll research the Burger Wars over the last few decades, you'll see that McDonald's started distancing themselves in the burger race when they added one amenity. What do you think that was? Hint: it wasn't the McRib!

It was the Playground.

This move showed—more than any McDonald's menu innovation—that the big boys and girls behind the Golden Arches understood their core audience: busy moms and dads who don't always have time to cook for their kids. It showed they understood their target audience's needs and wants.

After they pick their kids up from school, parents need a quick meal—maybe to tide them over until dinner. Parents can watch their kids play while they unwind from work, catch up on quick phone calls, or chat with other parents.

To this day if you ask a kid what they want to eat, he or she will not respond, "a hamburger" or "chicken nuggets," but instead will say, "McDonald's."

This phenomenon underscores one of the greatest lessons I learned from reading Dan Kennedy's first booklet and subsequent works. When people associate your brand with your category, you have achieved superbrand status. In other words, the fact that kids ask for McDonald's when their parents ask them "what" they want to eat, cements McDonald's as the undisputed king of fast food in their audience's minds.

Marketing Like Mickey D

Now, the extension of branding is marketing. They're close cousins for sure.

Building distinction into your leadership brand is critical to your success as a leader. Every opportunity you get to show your ability to lead puts your brand on display. Every chance you get to lead adds or detracts from your marketing campaign for additional leadership opportunities.

While McDonald's practice of giving kids a toy with their Happy Meals has come under fire as "inappropriate marketing," it's still filed in my mind as brilliant marketing even if you don't agree with the practice. Detractors feel that by giving kids a toy, kids develop a loyalty to McDonald's that creates an unhealthy connection between the corporation and the child. No matter where you are on the issue, I want to use this example to reiterate why developing your leadership brand is so important.

HOW TO ARCHITECT YOUR LEADERSHIP BRAND

Every great brand started with a leader who, along with his or her team, came up with what's known as the brand's Values Statement, what you strive for or stand for.

So we can't talk about you becoming a leader or a better leader until you are first crystal clear on your values statement.

General Electric, whose motto is "imagination at work," is a diversified company with $163 billion in annual revenue. Its leaders are encouraged—no, expected—to consistently come up with imaginative and innovative ways to serve their core audiences.

Lexus's credo is the Pursuit of Perfection. Lexus car owners know they're going to get the white-glove treatment. If they bring in their cars for service, they know they'll get a Lexus loaner to drive until theirs is fixed.

The National Basketball Association's (NBA) newest campaign, "Bigger than basketball" features various commercials where the biggest stars on the planet are shown giving back to their communities. Consumer goods giant, Procter & Gamble, scored big with its Mother's Day commercial, showing mothers as having the most important job on Earth.

You get the point: Your leadership style and brand should reflect the values you embody as well as an understanding of those who follow you.

What Are Your Values?

_____

_____

_____

Now that you've crystallized your values, it's time to start building a rock-solid leadership brand. This requires six key actions that you'll be able to complete with even greater fortitude once you've completed the book.

> #1: Decide to become a great leader. (Yes, it is a decision.)
> #2: Develop your unique leadership strategy.
> #3: Evaluate your leadership assets and blind spots, which we'll address in the next section, Psychology of Leadership.
> #4: Invest in your own leadership development.
> #5: Ask for responsibilities that put you in leadership and co-leadership roles.
> #6: Track your progress and continue to develop.

Don't Lead until You're Ready

If you think about it, you can make the best widget in the world, but if no one knows about it, it's not the best widget in the world. By the same token if you're trying to push yourself as a leader before you're actually a person people will follow, you won't have much success either.

There's an old saying: If a tree falls in the forest and no one is there to hear it, does it make a sound? In the same respect, if you make the best burger in the world, but nobody eats it, is it the best burger in the world? Maybe, but if no one knows, it doesn't matter! The flip side of that could look like this: Your burger's bad and you spend millions of dollars trying to get people to come through the door, but when they taste your burger, they don't come back or tell their friends about it, so you've just wasted a million marketing dollars.

I don't know which scenario you fall into today, but I'd be willing to bet that you're either a leader who's looking to hone your skills so that you can get more followers, more promotions, more influence, and more money, or you're a wannabe leader who thinks he's ready to lead but doesn't have a brand worth following ... yet.

Let's say you're a man and you're trying to get a date. There's a party coming up, and the woman you've had your eye on for a few months is attending. You put on your best suit. You get your hair done just right. You floss. You get your shoes shined. You shave your unibrow. Everything is perfect. It's showtime. You walk into the room and all the lights are off. She can't see all the work you've put into looking and smelling good. Does it matter?

Clearly, focusing on the product is important, but if you spend 200 hours perfecting the product or service and only two hours making people aware of it, you're not going to be in business very long. And if you are, the guys down the street, who are constantly marketing, are gonna kick your butt.

HERE'S THE OTHER SIDE OF THE COIN.

You're new to the company and the CEO has taken a liking to you. She's told you that you've got the potential to one day be the CEO yourself. You get pumped. You're fired up. And the following week at the annual sales conference you start spouting off about what you'd do if you were in charge of a certain division within the company. Pretty soon the buzz is that this loud-mouth kid's an arrogant you-know-what. Guess what? You've likely damaged your leadership prospects in that company. All because you weren't ready to lead, and worse, you violated the Love Them and Lead Them recommended order for creating leadership success.

- Create a magnetic brand.
- Understand the psychology of amazing leaders.
- Communicate and connect effectively.
- Build phenomenal influence.

Most leaders fall into leadership by accident, and sometimes they simply get baptized by fire. In the example above, the new executive just got a little ahead of himself because he was excited that a bigwig noticed his "potential." Remember, potential means nothing if you don't follow up with the right approach, attitude, and work ethic.

Now, some would-be leaders think that just by "working hard" they can become leaders. Nothing can be further from the truth. Those people focus on their own skill set. They focus on getting an Executive MBA; they focus on their Six Sigma Training or their ability to crunch numbers and make financial projections, and they assume these things will make them a successful leader because people want to follow successful people, right? Sorta.

You see, you can be the most successful person in the room, but if no one on your team likes or respects you, or more importantly, listens to you, you're just like that delicious hamburger I mentioned earlier. You're a good-looking woman in a room full of eligible men but the lights are off.

That humid day in the spring of 2009, as I sat in my driveway reevaluating my life and business, my lights were off.

I'd spent a great deal of my adult life carving myself into a near-perfect businessman. I was extraordinarily busy, though when I think about it, not very productive. Most days I looked like I'd been plucked from the pages of Esquire, but inside I felt like a plucked chicken. I'd developed an athlete's discipline around building my sales and business skills.

But as I sat in my driveway that evening after work, about to head into the house where silence goes to die, it hit me. I was a good person, with great intentions. Yet two options were still staring me square in the face: I could continue doing what I was doing, and getting the same results. Or I could face the bitter truth that I had become a terrible leader and start dealing with what was certain to be one of toughest comebacks of my life.

"Leadership Is as Leadership Does."

~ What Forrest Gump would have said if he were a leadership trainer.

PART I:
THE PSYCHOLOGY
OF LEADERSHIP

If there was a Ph.D for Leadership Hard Knocks, I'd have a big ol' certificate hanging on my wall right now. Learning to love and respect people was something I had to learn the hard way. Over the past 20 years I've developed what most would call a dominant leadership personality because I believed it was the best way to achieve my goals. You know what I'm talking about—be a go-getting bull in the china shop if it means getting what you want. That was me.

Unfortunately, after burning many critical bridges in many different relationships, I've had to reevaluate my position on leadership. After losing thousands of dollars and spending countless hours frustrated and upset because my organization wasn't growing at the rate I thought it should, I finally learned the importance of relationships. And boy, did those lessons come with a few scrapes and burns I'll happily share with you throughout the book.

Like me, many leaders have a natural proclivity to be a bit headstrong. You probably always think you're right, don't you? Even if we don't say it out loud, most of us think it. You also probably feel somewhat gifted and may often wonder why you were blessed to be so much more advanced than those around you. Am I reading anybody's mail right now?

All of that confidence is good; as a matter of fact, it's great, but don't let the confidence go to your head. Being right isn't what marks a great leader. Humility and honor do. Learn from my mistakes. Avoid some of the landmines I stepped onto. If the saying "we teach what we've learned or need to learn" is true, I'm certainly on my way to becoming a master of leadership. At least I hope so. As you read the pages of this book, learn from me, yes, but also take a good long look in the mirror and ask yourself, "How can I use these lessons and this information to become a better leader today?" Let's learn a bit more about the psychology of leaders.

WHERE DOES LEADERSHIP COME FROM?

Are leaders born? Or are leaders made? That's the question that's been asked for centuries. The answer is clear: It's probably both. A person can develop the characteristics of great leaders early in their lives, but were they born with those traits? We'll never know. We can't actually dissect DNA for the leadership gene.

We don't really know if great leaders were born to lead or if those qualities were nurtured along the way—or if it's some combination of the two. Most leaders would like to believe they were leaders from the time they exited their mother's womb, but again, I'm not so sure about that. And honestly, does it even matter?

Most leadership behavior starts at an early age. Research bears that out. Yet the definition of leadership carries so many different connotations that it's almost impossible to nail down what's leadership and what's simple behavioral or personality dominance.

For instance, when a first-grade teacher tells his or her students to line up at the door for lunch, is the kid who barges his or her way to the front of the line a leader or a bully? Or is the kid who gets the other kids into a specific line formation the leader? Or is the leader actually the kid who recognizes that it doesn't matter how they line up because the teacher's going to change it anyway? You see my point? Leadership is in the eye of the beholder. It depends on how you view leadership.

I do believe, however, that leaders know the value in being adaptable. They understand that leadership calls for the ability to change and adjust based on what's needed in the situation. The term *leadership*, however, suggests that you're out front. That you're representing a group or team. This means you've been ordained to speak for the group in certain circumstances and those following you have endorsed your position within the group.

Were you born to lead or built to lead? Doesn't matter. If you want to be a successful leader in any capacity—at work, at church, at home, in your community, or on your team—there are three things you must do: love, understand, and respect those who have decided to follow you. Without them, you're a hotdog bun without a wiener. A kite without a sail. Without them, you're simply talking loud but saying nothing.

Like, understand, respect. Put those three words in a vault and commit them to memory. They are the keys to leadership success.

Now ... repeat after me ...

If people don't like me, they won't follow me.

If people don't respect me, they will not follow me.

If they think I don't understand them, they won't follow me.

23

And if they don't like, respect, and trust me, I will never have influence with them.

LOVE'S LAW OF LEADERSHIP

Law of Respect

Everyone wants respect, and no one wants to be disrespected or disrespectful.

R-E-S-P-E-C-T

Any productive relationship starts with respect. So let's examine my Law of Respect, which says that everyone wants respect, and no one wants to be disrespected or disrespectful.

So, when communicating with a person about offensive behavior, include the topic of respect in the conversation. The word strikes a powerful chord with most people. If you have a person who's violated a core value of the organization, try this approach: "Our organization has operated on these principles for the last 20 years, and I firmly believe this has made us the industry leader. Therefore, we feel strongly about everyone being in compliance. I'm optimistic that you can respect that."

Now who's going to say, "No, actually I want to be disrespectful"?

I also use this Law in my listing presentations. Most homeowners want me to come right in and go over the numbers. "How much will my house sell for?" they want to know. However, history has taught me that before I start diving into the numbers, I first need to sell myself because if the price isn't what they wanted to hear, they're not going to listen to one word out of my mouth.

Once I've effectively conveyed my expertise, I'll have credibility to share my suggested sales price. So when I walk in and they ask, "How much can you get for us?" I respond by saying, "It's been my experience that in order for us to decide this relationship's a good fit for us both, we need to lay the ground rules for the transaction so that you know what my expectations are, and I know yours. I find that doing it this way creates a smoother transaction and ultimately both parties win. Hopefully you can respect that."

In my nearly 10-year long real estate career, no seller's ever responded, "Just give me the numbers." Why? Because if they did, that would be disrespectful.

You see, no matter how hard you try to lead them, if respect isn't at the top of your list of qualities, you will not be successful at leading. No matter how much you attempt to impose your will, manipulate the situation, or market yourself as a leader, they won't follow you.

So what actually makes people follow leaders? Well, that's what Mr. Maslow's about to help us understand.

WHAT DO FOLLOWERS WANT AND NEED?

In 1943, Abraham Maslow developed what we refer to today as Maslow's Hierarchy of Needs. It studies human innate behavior, based on their needs. In an attempt to better understand human behavior and why we do what we do, he discovered there were five basic levels of human needs:

PHYSIOLOGICAL, SAFETY, LOVE / BELONGING, ESTEEM, AND SELF-ACTUALIZATION.

PHYSIOLOGICAL

These are primary and basic needs, necessary for life. Food, water, and air are examples of physiological needs. In one's quest for actualization, physiological needs must be addressed first.

SAFETY

Upon satisfying one's physiological needs, the next level of needs becomes active. Many adults pay little to no attention to these needs as they are taken for granted until they are thrust into times of calamity or chaos, when social structures break down. A classic example of this situation would be Californians in the midst of a natural disaster such as an earthquake. Safety is clearly of the utmost importance to these folks.

LOVE / BELONGING

When physiological and safety needs are met and are no longer inundating the minds of individuals, they are then free to pursue Love / Belonging. People desire to overcome feelings of loneliness and alienation and begin to seek the place where they fit in. At this level they are able to give and receive love and find a sense of belonging.

ESTEEM

Esteem needs begin to emerge once the other three levels of needs are satisfied. People need a stable and high regard for themselves as well as respect for others. Upon meeting these needs, one becomes self-confident and feels like an asset to the world.

ACTUALIZATION

After all of these needs are met, it is then that an individual's desire for self-actualization begins to manifest. Maslow describes this as being freed or released to do what you were created or born to do. One important thing to understand about Maslow's theory is that it is a hierarchy, which means each need builds upon the next. So, although love and belonging are needs, you won't even recognize or desire to fulfill this need until the two more primary needs have been addressed.

Let me give you a practical example to show you how this works. Most of you reading this book are probably stuck somewhere between Levels 3 and 4, love / belonging and esteem. We all desire relationships, to give and receive love, and to have a healthy esteem. That's why we engage in behavior to assist us in addressing these needs.

For example, we all take showers or baths, we brush our teeth, and we comb our hair. Why? Because we know that if we're going to be able to have meaningful relationships and have a healthy esteem, we can't smell bad, we can't have bad breath, and we can't sport hair that looks like we just got out of bed, right?

Now let's look at a situation like Hurricane Katrina. Surviving a catastrophic event like a hurricane tends to shift our needs. The primary concern would be finding loved ones or finding, food, water, and shelter, but it would not be personal hygiene. You and the individuals you lead have these innate needs. When conflict arises, everyone's needs change. Depending upon the type of organization you lead, the needs the people may be trying to meet will be different. A six- or seven-figure earner might not have the same concerns as the $12/hour factory worker in the company.

If downsizing happens, you can bet that those working under you will have a different level of anxiety about their job security than you do. You'll also have to be in tune with what those needs are on the spot. I didn't understand this early in my career.

Understanding Maslow's Hierarchy of Needs changed everything for me. It made me a more influential leader by providing insights into human psychology and behavior that goes beyond the surface. Now I'm still a work in progress, but I'm also starting to understand not only what drives folks to follow and remain loyal to certain leadership styles but also how great leaders continue to reengineer themselves for greater efficiency and effectiveness.

LEADERSHIP

Getting people to willingly do what they would not ordinarily do.

Leadership Is as Leadership Feels

Although "strong" leadership is often viewed in terms associated with masculine energy, the foundation for good leadership is steeped firmly in valuing people and relationship building, qualities associated with feminine energy. Not only do great leaders understand the importance of relationships, they become good at cultivating them. They never forget that people are people, not machines. They don't lose sight of the fact that people are only one part physical; they are also emotional, spiritual, psychological, and mental beings. That's why great leaders are often perceived to be charismatic. They never forget that human connection is paramount to effective leadership.

Take former president Bill Clinton, one of the most popular and well-liked former US presidents in our history. Though I've never met him, if you read articles or features on him, you'll almost always see him described as "likable." If you look at archived videos of him interacting with people, you'll see how well he connects on a simple human level with everyone he encounters.

Being president is a high-powered job, and Clinton certainly had a few well-publicized distractions during his terms, but if you ever caught a television clip of him in a crowd of thousands of people, you would've seen that he had a way of making people feel like they were the only thing on his mind in that moment. Bill Clinton loves, yes, loves people. It showed. It still does. He knows that people want and need to feel special. As a leader, his ability to make people feel special makes him one of the most endearing figures in our nation's history. He understood it well: If you don't love them, you can't lead them.

GOOD MARKETING STARTS WITH GOOD RELATIONSHIPS

Although the Dan Kennedy book that my mentor, Jonathan, gave me provided the swift kick in the butt I needed, I still had to take a few steps back. If I were going to be successful, I had some work to do in the area of personal development. I would need to understand that marketing is nothing more than an extension of the *relationship* between seller and buyer. Therefore, it's highly emotional.

Now, most men don't like to think they need any of what they think is "touchy feely" stuff, and if that's been your perception of personal growth, I'm going to challenge you to change the lens you're looking through.

First, I'm curious about who you consider leaders in today's marketplace.

When I say the word leader, what are some of the names that come to mind? Depending on your age, different names will surface: Churchill. Jobs. Stewart. Obama. Zuckerberg. Winfrey. What qualities come to mind when you think of these individuals? Charisma. Innovation. Communicators.

We tend to think that successful people are leaders simply because we believe it takes leadership to be successful. But what's the most basic quality essential to successful leadership? It's the ability to relate to and understand the needs and desires of those who follow you. Understanding that one, single principle will not only transform you personally but also your bank account.

Wait. Is Jerome Love saying there's a connection between leadership and marketing? That's exactly what Jerome Love is saying! Effective marketing and leadership are both predicated on relating to people and understanding their needs and wants.

As I said earlier, marketing is an extension of the relationship between seller and buyer. People buy because they believe the product seller or brand can solve their problem. That's why they choose one brand over another one.

Likewise, in leadership, people follow leaders because they believe that leader will take them to the promised land, whatever that might be. In companies the "promised land" might be bigger profits or fatter margins. In relationships the carrot might be a deeper connection or a successful family. In athletic settings, the prize might be a championship.

Like marketing, leadership is a highly emotional relationship that is akin to the earlier example of kids asking their parents to take them to McDonald's. If you have kids, you know exactly what I'm talking about. They have a physical reaction to going—or not going—to McDonald's because of the strong *relationship* they have with the brand.

WHAT DOES IT TAKE TO BE A SUCCESSFUL LEADER?

There are many ways to take an inventory of where you stand as a leader or a potential leader. In fact, great leadership consists of one part traits and one part skills.

Let's talk traits first. This is what I call the Love Them and Lead Them Leaderboard. It consists of seven key traits and the four key skills that most successful people possess—even those who don't consider themselves leaders.

TRAITS: Rank yourself in these 11 categories on a scale of 1 (low) to 5 (high).

_____**Accountable:** assumes responsibility for contribution to outcomes

_____**Competitive**: desires to play at the game's highest level

_____**Enthusiasm:** participates with vigor and energy

_____**Generous:** willing to share the work, credit, and recognition

_____**Passion:** tenacity in the direction of the team's goals

_____**Transparency:** no desire to hide flaws or faults

_____**Visionary:** can see and convey long-term possibilities to the team

SKILLS: The most critical skills that every leader practices are

- Relationship building   _____

- Problem solving   _____

- Conflict resolution   _____

- Relatability   _____

TOTAL SCORE: _____

WHAT DOES YOUR SCORE MEAN?

A perfect score, which nobody who's honest or truly self-aware ever scores, is 55. Nevertheless, your score should reveal the areas where you need the most work and should encourage you to develop a plan for strengthening that part of the assessment.

LEADER TRAITS:

Scores between 28 and 35: Good job, you're on the right track. Fine-tune your lower scores and keep strengthening your high ones.

Scores between 20 and 27: You're likely fluctuating back and forth in your mind and heart as to whether you can stand the heat in the leader's kitchen. Make a decision to lead and you'll see the difference in how people respond to you.

Scores between 12 and 19: A great commitment is required to get to the level where peers will respect your voice and talent to lead.

Scores 11 and below: At this point it doesn't appear you've embraced all that's required to lead.

LEADER SKILLS

Scores between 16 and 20: Way to go! You've worked on the behaviors of successful leaders. Keep looking in the mirror.

Scores between 10 and 15: Fortunately, developing skills is a matter of practicing the right behaviors. Get a coach or mentor to show you the ropes but keep practicing.

Scores between 5 and 9: There is lots of work to be done, but balance this score with the "traits" score to see if you're truly cut out for the tough roads leaders travel.

Scores 4 and below: Focus exclusively on building your personal growth foundations of self-image, esteem, and confidence right now.

IDENTIFYING YOUR LEADERSHIP PROFILE

There are tons of indices and profile assessments that attempt to help us understand who we are and why we behave the way we do at home, work, or play. Some of the more well-known ones are DISC© or the Meyers-Briggs© Personality Indicator.

These inventories or assessments are not tools to be used to judge people for their differences but rather to help us leverage those differences. They reveal that regardless of where you were born, raised, or lived, most of us have unique drivers, things that explain why we do what we do in any given situation.

In fact, when you read about great Hollywood actors, you'll sometimes hear them talk about their "motivation" for their characters. This refers to what's driving their characters to do the things they do and say the things they say. Many psychologists have broken human motivation into two main categories: pain and pleasure.

In other words, we're typically either pursuing pleasure or avoiding pain. Though not necessarily true in every case, the potential experience of pain typically overshadows the potential to experience pleasure, which sometimes explains human behavior.

Hippocrates is widely regarded as the father of modern medicine. One of his most famous studies included the study of body fluids called "humors." He theorized that human moods, emotions, and behaviors were caused by these humors. Through his studies he developed the first typology of temperament and linked emotional behavior, mental capacity, and moral attitude to four distinct and different categories: **Sanguine, Choleric, Melancholy, and Phlegmatic.**

I offer these temperament types to you so that you can not only identify yourself but also begin to identify your colleagues', family members', and teammates' temperaments for the purpose of creating more productive and more effective relationships.

Sanguine: This personality type is highly extroverted. They love to be at social gatherings, making new friends; however, they also have a tendency to be very sensitive. Sanguines are notorious for being habitually late, and their worst fear is social rejection.

Choleric: These are your doers, the Type A personality. They have lots of ambition and energy, and they try to instill those same behaviors in others. Cholerics are known for their aggression and natural tendency to dominate and, as a result, are not very sensitive to other people's needs. Most of your great military and political leaders fall into this category. Their worst fear is being taken advantage of.

Melancholy: This personality is your perfectionist. They are very information driven. To them, information is everything and they see no gray; everything is black or white. Many accountants, doctors, and individuals in other analytical professions fall into this category. They have a proclivity toward depression as they never feel like things are right, and their worst fear is being wrong.

Phlegmatic: These are your shy personalities; they are very introverted and typically very kind and compassionate toward others. This group looks to avoid conflict even at their own expense. Experts suggest this group is most likely to "go postal" as they have a tendency to hold things inside until they explode. They are very consistent; they enjoy personal friendships and alone time, and their worst fear is change.

WHO ARE YOU?

Now, here's what interesting: Most people are not just one profile. You can be a mash-up of several profiles, a Choleric-Phlegmatic or a Choleric-Melancholy. Personalities are never purely any one type; that's what makes human beings so fascinating.

But because understanding your followers is such an integral part of successful leadership, it certainly behooves you to know (1) who you are and what motivates you, and (2) who's on your team and what motivates them.

So go ahead and take a moment to identify yourself and those closest to you at home and at work so that you can start communicating better for great influence.

AT HOME

You:

Spouse:

Children:

AT WORK:

Team Leader:

Coworker:

Coworker:

Coworker:

If you need a refresher, flip back to the Hippocrates's index and see if you nailed the profiles for your employees or team members. Leverage the information to become more accepting and more productive. Have some fun with it!

Hypocrite or Hippocrates?

In the fall of 1997 as a junior in college at The University of Texas at Austin, I joined Alpha Phi Alpha Fraternity, Inc. One of the things that attracted me to this organization was its members' commitment to service and program diversity. Being an Alpha truly challenged me to learn how to work with others on a team, and our fraternity was largely relationally driven, which as you know by now, was not my strong suit.

At that point in my life, I had not learned about Hippocrates's personality profiles, and I kind of assumed that everyone thought and operated the same way that I did. As members of the same fraternity, at minimum I assumed we all shared the same values. And I certainly didn't think people with different approaches and personality profiles could successfully work together. I couldn't have been more wrong on that point.

Right off the bat I began to have run-ins with the older frat brothers as a result of my inability to work with people effectively or, from my perspective, their inability to work with me. It never dawned on me that this was one of my leadership blind spots. I just thought it was a clash of personalities.

Here's a prime example: We'd have an event on Friday night that was to begin at ten o'clock. The spoken rule was that everyone was to arrive an hour ahead of time. Too many times I'd show up at nine and no one else would be there. Everyone else would stroll in between 9:15 all the way to 9:35. This didn't work for me. In fact, it drove me crazy.

So naturally, when they'd finally arrive, the first thing I'd do is tear into them for being late. After I'd finished my punctuality lecture, I'd give them their assignment, dismiss them, and expect them to joyfully carry out their orders.

From my perspective, you knew the rule, you broke the rule, you deserve a punishment. If you haven't figured it out yet, I am naturally a Choleric personality with a lot of Melancholy tendencies. My Melancholy saw black and white, right and wrong; there was no gray.

Needless to say, I was not nominated for the Most Fraternal Brother Award. Nor was I very effective as a leader within the organization because people did not like me. They categorized me as un-fraternal because I was more into rules than being social or relational. It's funny. I thought "being about the business" actually made me an exceptional leader—someone who cared mostly about "getting it done." Clearly I had a lot to learn, and because I could be a rockhead, you already know that things are going to get worse for me before they get better.

My initial response was, "To heck with them, I can do it myself." And that's exactly what I attempted to do. This is the same approach most self-employed individuals take. I'm sure many of my fellow Cholerics out there are saying, "Right on, you did the right thing" or "You were right." But it's not about being right or wrong; it's about being effective, I later learned the hard way.

You can't be effective as a leader if you believe in the philosophy, "If you want something done right, you got to do it yourself!" Trust me, I tried it and it doesn't work. It's a faulty belief that's steeped in ego, fear, and selfishness.

So, you have a choice. You can be right or you can be successful. If you haven't figured it out already, I opted for being right waaaaaay too long. If you're still being a hard-head who likes saying, "See, I was right," keep reading.

RELATING = RESULTS

It's a simple formula. Relating = results. But when you think about that phrase, it sounds relatively simple: relating to others. Playing well with others. Team building. Pretty vague concepts that we all typically nod in understanding to when we hear them, but do we really understand what it means to relate to others? What in the world is that?

I'm with you. How do I know, as leader, if I'm indeed relating well to my team? It's simple. Lean in a bit closer. Here it comes.

The way you know if you're relating to (reaching) your team is by looking at the Big R: **results.**

Is your team winning? Are you improving? Progressing? Transforming? If your team's not doing any of those four things, no, you're not relating to others as a leader must. So, you ask, "How can I ensure that my team's doing these four things?" Become the leader that earns their respect and has their best interests at heart. Those aren't just pretty words on a page either. If you don't respect your followers, they won't follow you. If you don't genuinely have their best interests at heart, they'll know it. You can't fool them. They'll see right through you.

Some of us confuse "relating to" with "getting along with." They're not the same. Relating in leadership terms may not always translate into being liked or loved in the moment because honestly, sometimes leaders have to make some difficult decisions that don't feel good for them or their followers. Leading will often mean you're behaving and speaking in a language to your team that translates into subsequent behavior that's going in the direction you want: Higher levels of productivity. Fatter margins. Fewer customer complaints. Bigger profits.

Let's face it: The journey to growing a successful business or relationship isn't fun every single minute of the day. I'm never going to tell you that great leadership is a picnic, and anybody who says so is lying. Thankfully great leadership isn't about creating a Disneyland environment; it's about creating a culture where people are inspired to do great things because your leadership makes them want to come to work and get great results.

Leadership's Not a Popularity Contest

When I was in high school, it wasn't uncommon for the president of the class to be the quarterback on the football team or the prettiest girl in the school. It wasn't necessarily about leadership qualities all the time. Now, I'm not saying the quarterback wasn't a great leader on the field, but was he really the best person to lead the junior class? Maybe, maybe not.

But understand that this "popularity" mentality is still at work in companies and organizations today, which leads me to ask an important question: "How does the 'Hunk of the High School' get voted president when he's not the most qualified to do the job?"

Leadership is a lot about "relatability"—how much folks identify with you. This is a critical piece of the puzzle, so don't rush through this part. The hunky quarterback is relatable and likeable not because people can actually relate to what

40

he DOES. Heck, most of us will never be able to do what he does with the football, but he's relatable because they "want to." They want to be masters at their craft or ability. They want the adoration and adulation star athletes or celebrities get. So they often transfer their positive desires to have what the Hunk has into great followership. Make sense? Leading is partly about being someone people want to be like or emulate in some way.

It's a powerful leadership quality to possess that sometimes explains why very capable executives have a difficult time leading their teams. If your team doesn't admire or want to be like you or have what you have, you can't lead them. Period.

UNDERSTANDING THEIR NEEDS

I'm always amazed by how much we take for granted. Children take their parents for granted. Parents take their children for granted. Execs take their employees for granted. Retailers take their customers for granted. Yet where would we be without each other? I couldn't be a parent without my kids. I wouldn't be a husband without my wife. Your company would perish without its customers.

So when a customer buys your product, service, or program, that act shouldn't be taken lightly. You don't exist without them. And when you stop and think about it like that, it's pretty sobering. Sobering enough to challenge you to treat them with more respect and dignity.

Now let's take a quick break and reflect on why this section was important: I wanted to help you embrace the fact that leadership should not be approached as a chance to inflate your ego, your sense of entitlement, or your celebrity status, but rather to start seeing leading as the highest honor in the land.

DUMP THE BOSS MENTALITY

Too many supervisors think they're leaders, and many are not. Too many would-be-great supervisors are stuck in "I'm in charge" hell. It's been said, a leader with no followers is simply taking a stroll. You do not choose to lead people. People choose to follow. Your title does not make you a leader. It may give you a reason to brag to your buddies or add a few extra letters after your name, but until people start following you, you're not really a leader.

We use tons of words interchangeably: Coach. Mentor. Leader. Manager. Supervisor. So let's break them all down and put them in their proper perspective. First, you've got to abandon the hierarchy paradigm, where you see the world as a pyramid. Boss on top. Subordinates on the bottom. Lots of organizational charts still resemble pyramids. Lose that way of seeing your team. Just set it on fire right now. It doesn't work any longer. I'm not sure it ever did.

What do I mean by hierarchy hell? Those folks who are so married to their position in the company that they forget to lead. There's a great line in the movie *The American President* where Michael Douglas, portraying the US president, says he was so busy trying to keep his job he forgot to DO his job. That's most executives in the world. They're so busy trying not to lose favor with their "uppers" they forget they're in a leadership role to actually lead.

As a result of leading by hierarchy, many potentially good or great leaders crumble because nobody's following them. When I conduct leadership trainings, I'll demonstrate how this works. I pick two people and tell them to stand up. I then tell them they're leaders. Then I pick four or five people and tell them to follow only one of the people I picked as leaders.

Each leader then has to do certain things, such as take five steps forward, lift your right arm, etc. Both "leaders" do the same things, yet only one of the leaders actually has people behind him (followers). Then I ask the group, "Which of these two folks is the leader?" and they almost immediately pick the person everyone followed. Now both did the exact same actions; however, only one was seen as the leader. Why? Because he was the only one with followers. If you have followers, you will also have influence.

A few years ago renowned rapper 50 Cent (aka Curtis Jackson) logged onto his Twitter account and sent out a simple tweet endorsing a consumer product. That week, the product's stock skyrocketed and many of 50 Cent's Twitter followers went out and bought the product at record levels. Is that leadership or influence? Why?

_____

_____

_____

Renowned leadership expert John Maxwell said leadership is about influence, a concept I'm eager to discuss in Part III of this book. A successful leader is a person that can get people to do things they ordinarily would not do and enjoy the process. If you desire to be a successful leader, you have to become influential. Successful influencers understand that one's ability to influence is not initiated by themselves, but those they desire to influence. These concepts will continue to crystallize in your mind as we continue down the Love Them and Lead Them path. Let's turn our attention to the business of leadership.

"If they don't buy you, they won't buy the product."

THE BUSINESS OF LEADERSHIP

A prudent business owner's number one objective is to figure out what his potential customers want—not need. If you desire to be a successful leader that people are magnetically drawn to and one they want to follow, you have to think and function like a business. Just as a leader must have followers in order to be considered a leader, for a business to survive, it must have customers, people who are willing to support or purchase the business's products or service.

Most people will tell you that you need to uncover your prospect's needs. I say needs almost always come second to wants. But how can that be? Think about the car you drive. Is that the car you need to drive or *want* to drive? If money were no object and you were given the chance to walk onto any car lot in the world, pick the car of your choice, and drive it off the lot, free and clear, which dealership would you head to?

Would you get the sensible $10,000 Honda Civic or would you drive at near breakneck speed to get to the Ferrari or Hummer dealership? You probably wouldn't say, "Well, I've got millions of dollars; I think I'll get a pre-owned Nissan Sentra." Would you? Probably not. Now, do you *need* a Ferrari? No, but you're likely to be highly motivated to buy one given the opportunity and funds to do so.

Consumer behavior is much more wants-oriented than needs-oriented. Influential leaders are masters at understanding and appealing to people's wants, while taking care of their needs. Leaders who can communicate to their customers or prospects that they understand their concerns, cares, desires, and needs will ultimately not only get to lead those people but also have great influence in their lives.

Let's take the presidential election. It doesn't matter which years you choose; just pick one. The candidate that is more effective at conveying to voters that their pain, their wants, and their needs have been heard almost always wins.

Political elections are highly charged, emotionally draining events. People want to be heard. They want to trust their candidate. They need to believe that the guy or gal they're voting for is going to do right by them. The guy or gal that wins has the most influence, period. He or she may not be the best candidate for the job, but whoever said the best always wins, lied.

Take the 2004 Democratic presidential bid. Clearly then-Senator Hillary Clinton was politically more qualified than then-Senator Barack Obama. She has the makings of a pedigree of a potential commander in chief. What she didn't have that Obama did have was off-the-charts likeability and relatability. She simply wasn't able to connect emotionally with constituents, and it cost her the chance to run for president that year.

SELLING YOURSELF AS A LEADER

As I said, you don't get to decide that you're going to lead a group of people; the people do. However, that shouldn't stop you from lobbying for the job! If you think you possess enough of the qualities and skills to improve lives or bottom lines, by all means, go for it. However, you'll have to market yourself like you mean it to convince folks you should be chosen over all the other options in the market or company.

Your leadership brand is one that must be crafted with clarity and care. So let's tap into your profile real quick. Answer these five questions:

1. Why do you want to be a leader?

2. How do you think people perceive you?

3. Why would people follow you?

4. What's unique about your leadership promise that would make you stand out?

5. Do you care more about the people or the results?

Do you want to be a leader for selfish reasons, such as so that you can tell people what to do or so that people will look up to you? If so, I suggest you keep it moving. You won't be a very good leader because your motivation is self-centered.

When asked how people perceive them, most people have a very high regard for themselves. I don't want to burst your bubble, but you should probably come down out of the clouds and realize that many folks are eager to dive into the negative end of the pool. I'm not saying you're not a terrific person; I'm simply suggesting that you not go crazy with an inflated opinion of yourself, otherwise you may be tempted to tank the moment you hear negative feedback from a follower.

Why would people follow you? There's only one reason and I said it earlier: because they believe you can help them get what they want. That's it. Don't kid yourself. They are not following you because they think you're cool. They're following you because they think you're the one to solve their problem.

What's unique about your leadership promise that would make prospects choose to follow you? That's the good old

USP question—unique selling proposition. What makes you so different or worthy of my vote? To be able to communicate this difference, you've actually got to know what other leaders are doing—and not doing.

Do you care more about people or results? I love this one. When I do leadership training, the room's almost always split down the middle on this question. People argue that if you lose sight of the results and get poor results, you won't get to lead. The other half says if you don't show people that you care, they won't help you get the results.

Guess what? Both are right. Sorta. You see, great leaders are masters at getting followers invested in achieving results. You can't shove results down folks' throats; you have to make the process, the journey of getting the results so emotionally satisfying that your followers want to achieve them. That's the secret sauce.

Remember, leadership's emotional *and* it's relational. If your people feel connected to, respected by, and cared for by you, they'll enthusiastically be about the results, which in turn will strengthen your leadership status.

Leaders joyfully give center stage to the other players. They're confident that their behind-the-scenes work will be central to the success of the team even if they get none of the credit.

YOU, A LEADER?

There's nothing funnier (and maybe even sadder) than watching someone "try" to be a leader. It's painful actually. You've probably seen this phenomenon in action. I see it in sports all the time. A team comes together in practice, and the loudest person on the team starts shouting orders and attempting to establish the "hierarchy" on the team. Look at me! *Listen to me! I'm a leader!*

But the more you try to take over and force people to listen to and respect you, the less they actually do. Strange, huh? That's because leadership's not something you can force onto people. Oh, sure, they may do what you say out of submission or fear, but that's not leadership; that's a dictatorship. And that ultimately leads to a mighty fall. Again, ask Hitler.

So my charge with this book is to help you find your leadership flow. The style that's not only unique to you but also natural for you. To do that, we have to go back to something Dan Kennedy taught me.

Pizza in 30 Minutes ... or It's Free

That's the unique selling proposition that helped Domino's pizza revolutionize the pizza industry two decades ago.

Dan Kennedy delivers some of the best insights on USPs—unique selling propositions. He says it's one of the top three things every brand must figure out before it starts trying to "brand itself." If you don't know who you are, how are you going to get people to listen to what you have to say, or put another way, "buy what you're selling"? You can't.

Domino's was tired of watching other pizza companies steal their market share, so I'm sure they got together at a leadership retreat and asked some pretty hard questions. Questions that resulted in the "30 Minutes or Free" campaign during the '90s. That's what Domino's became known for, but who are *you?*

Let's do a warm-up exercise. This'll help you understand the importance of this discussion. Write the first company or brand that comes to mind when you see the words below.

Cough Syrup

Luxury Vehicle

Affordable Air Travel

MP3 Player

Athletic Shoes

Best NBA Player

Late Night Talk Show

Bathroom Tissue

Soft Drink

Toothpaste

Coffee House

Mexican Fast Food

Lotion

Video Sharing Site

Shampoo

Fast-Food Hamburgers

Grocery Store

Smartphone

Search Engine

The Law of Respect

Now, take a look at your answers. The USPs of the brands you listed have done such a great job of figuring out who they are and marketing that identity to you, that you think of them when you think of their *category*. Powerful concept, right?

Well, you don't need a $35 million annual advertising budget to be able to do the same. You simply need to know who you are and, most importantly, what your followers desire, what you bring to the table, and how to convey those assets in a way that excites people to want to follow you.

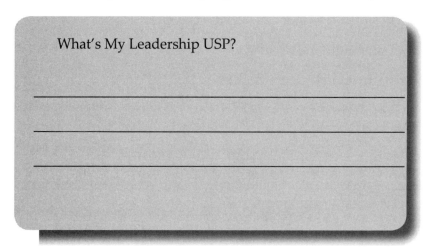

What's My Leadership USP?

_____

_____

_____

Above all, remember this: You're a walking, talking, living, breathing product with your own brand. Focus on developing marketing messages that convey your leadership USP on a daily basis. Ignore your marketing and you will be cast aside as quickly as all the other fads that did not stand the test of time!

AM I A HUNTER OR FISHER LEADER?

In my first book, *Get Up, Get Out & Get Something* (GU-GOGS™), I discuss a marketing strategy called Hunting versus Fishing. Most marketers fall into one of those categories. They either hunt or they fish. Hunters tend to go after their prey in an aggressive fashion, focusing on the "thrill of the kill." Fishermen, however, tend to take a more intelligent approach to catching fish. Fisherman study fish. They understand what fish like to eat, when they like to eat, what colors they're attracted to as well as what repels them. They know that if they understand the needs and wants of the fish, they'll ultimately draw the fish to them.

It's the same with successful leaders; they know the success or failure of their mission or cause is not about them. It's about those they lead. Just as the successful fisherman takes the time to study the fish, the successful leader studies his followers. He or she knows their likes and dislikes so that ultimately they can best accommodate the needs of their followers.

Take the successful sports movie *Remember the Titans*, which has multiple leadership themes we could use in this book. There's the leadership among the players on the football team. Leadership on the coaching staff. Town leadership and family leadership. It's a movie that's set during segregation, and for the first time black and white football players are about to share the same locker room and wear the same uniforms.

It's a divisive time in our history, and the new black head coach, played by Academy Award winner Denzel Washington, has some strong opinions about how to run the team—no matter what people think about him or his methods. His character, Boone, is so headstrong that his white assistant coach, Yoast, challenges him to remember that the season's not about him; it's about the players, the team.

It's a poignant moment because on one hand you can appreciate the passion Boone brings, yet on the other hand, Yoast has a point. Who's right? They're both right and they're both wrong. They are focused so much on proving the other wrong that at different times they both lose sight of what's really important: bringing these boys together to play as one and showing the racially divided town that blacks and whites can coexist harmoniously.

A good leader rarely forgets the big picture.

Part of the reason the Titan football players couldn't get on one accord is that their leaders weren't on the same page. It was hard for Boone or Yoast to persuade their team to stick together when they were divided. It'll be no different on your team. Can't preach what you're not modeling. So walk the walk.

SAY GOOD-BYE TO YOU

The next thing I'm going to ask you to do is die. I don't mean physically; I mean metaphorically. *You* have to die. You have to be willing to kill *yourself*. Now let me clarify. The essence of you is not a physical body. While your physical body is certainly a part of you, unless you're in a night club, people don't typically gravitate toward you—or navigate away from you, for that matter—based on your physical body.

They're more drawn to the real you, which is your inner being. This is comprised of your personality, demeanor, ideals, beliefs, values, mode of communication, etc. This is the real *you*. It is the you that makes people want to follow you enthusiastically or try to avoid you at all costs. And if your you is all about "Look at me. I'm important. I'm the one," you'll never be a great leader. Oh, sure, you may win some awards or get some big promotions, and you may even be well liked, but you'll never become a great leader.

The 2013 Super Bowl is a great illustration of how great leadership can elevate performance. Ray Lewis is not perfect. His history as a man is not without blemishes. But as a football player it's obvious his leadership elevated the Baltimore Ravens to new heights, especially during its 2013 run for the Super Bowl. In interviews, even his opponents, the guys who are paid to make sure his team loses, praised his leadership skills.

Let's examine why.

If we go back to my Leaderboard, we can see that Ray Lewis, at least from the outside looking in, possesses most, if not all of those traits. He's enthusiastic. He's passionate. He's a fierce competitor. He's quick to shower teammates with hugs and high fives. He's a magnet. Guys followed him.

Now, I've never been in the Ravens' locker room, but I know enough about leadership to be able to watch the Baltimore sideline during their 2013 playoff run and see how grown men responded to one of their own. The preacher, Ray Lewis, led his team to the promised land, behind the same principles I'm sharing with you right now.

Lewis, like so many other great leaders, may have started out being about himself, but as most of leaders have publicly admitted, at some point they had to die for their teams to be successful. You've got to let go of any and all preset ideals and beliefs and be open to consider the fact that maybe, as the saying goes, there is more than one way to skin a cat. If your ideals are hindering your team from succeeding, your ideals should die a swift death.

If the personality quirks you love are getting in the way of a productive business meeting, your quirks should be laid to rest. Notice the word consider. Maybe you don't have to die. Maybe you have it all together. Maybe those that work with you or follow your lead find it an absolute delight to be around you. Maybe they consistently turn in assignments on time and execute in a manner that pleases you 100 percent of the time. I guess anything is possible; I would consider that. If that's you, you can stop reading right now, shoot me an email me at Jerome@jeromelove.com and I'll send you a full refund.

Or if you're honest, you'll admit that you, too, are a work in progress. Let's keep this train moving ...

The stronger your relationship with your followers, the stronger their desire to help you succeed.

ALPHA LEADERSHIP

As I mentioned earlier, the idea for this book came about unfortunately because of the many bridges I've burned, many feelings I've hurt, and many relationships I've severed. As sobering as it is to admit that, it's also painful. I've been blessed to meet and work with some amazing folks, but some of them probably can't stand me to this day because of the way I behaved toward them. My grandmother always said, "A hard head makes a soft bottom." Only she didn't use the word "bottom."

During my junior semester at UT Austin, I also began the pledge process to join Alpha Phi Alpha Fraternity, Inc. Prior to joining I was filled with feelings of excitement, enthusiasm, and a great sense of admiration for the organization, as well as the members I'd see around campus.

These guys had it all together in my eyes and were darn near flawless. At the time the student body president was an Alpha. The head of the National Pan-Hellenic Council was an Alpha. The Alphas always had the best parties and certainly put on the best step shows. This was the fraternity for me, no question.

One day while looking through the Alpha history books, I found that many of the country's most notable and influential leaders were Alphas, such as Dr. Martin Luther King, Thurgood Marshall, and Jesse Owens, just to name a few. I knew this was the organization for me. So I began my pilgrimage to become a member of this elite group of men known around campus simply as the Alphas.

Being a neophyte, or newly initiated member, naturally I was energized and excited by what was about to become an exciting chapter in my life. I had joined this prestigious group of men that had it all together, and I admired what the organization stood for. I had visions of me waltzing into frat parties, stepping on stage at the annual Texas Revue, or giving the secret handshake to the prophytes, the more seasoned frat members. They were the old-school guys we neophytes or new members were expected to give a certain level of respect.

As a neophyte I could now attend our official chapter meetings, held on the first Sunday of every month at 3 p.m. This, by all accounts, was of dire importance to maintaining the level of quality programming and professionalism the men of Alpha Phi Alpha, Inc. exuded around campus. Our chapter meeting was the real deal. In order to enter, you first had to do the top-secret door knock followed by the members-only handshake. This was serious business! I was pumped.

The month after becoming a member, I was ready for my first meeting. I woke up early that Sunday morning and put on my best pair of dress pants, shirt, and tie. All meetings were formal attire. I had made arrangements to pick up my line brothers (LBs) at 1 p.m. so that we wouldn't be late. On time for me is at least 10 to 15 minutes early. Of course, I wanted to make a good impression. I was certain that my line brothers, given that they were highly professional, well-organized gentlemen, would want to be on time as well.

As the day progressed, everything was going according to plan. We arrived 10 minutes early, gave the secret door knock, and were greeted by our chapter vice president. Eager to greet my other fraternity brothers, I stepped through the door, only to see a long empty conference room table with chairs around it, also empty.

"Where *is* everyone?" I asked. It was now five minutes before meeting time. Everybody looked at me like I had a broccoli in my teeth. Nobody said a word.

They continued socializing while I grabbed my seat. I wanted to be ready when the meeting started at three o'clock. Much to my chagrin, the next person didn't arrive until 3:10. None of my other six pledge brothers were quite as rigid as I was apparently. So, even though it was now 15 minutes after our scheduled start time, they continued to shoot the breeze and chat about this and that, as though we weren't there on official business.

I finally blurted out in disgust, "Thought the meeting started at three."

One of my brothers shook his head and patted me on the back. "Relax, D dot," he said. "What's the rush?"

"D dot" was a nickname the prophytes had given me during the pledge process because my name is "Jerome D. Love," and the "D" is simply an initial. They thought that was hilarious, so they began to call me D dot.

Around 3:25 a few other prophytes showed up, and the meeting finally got underway. Truthfully I don't remember much of what happened in the meeting as I was beyond frustrated by this point. Frustrated because the meeting started nearly an hour late and no one seemed to care but me. I sat there pouting and disappointed that my frat brothers didn't hold punctuality in the highest regard, like I did. Disappointed that they seemed to look at me like I was the one with the problem. I didn't get it.

This was only the beginning of my leadership transformation. The year before I pledged, I'd met Aaron. He lived on my floor and seemed like a nice guy, though not someone I would probably hang out with. I'd see him every now and then and we'd speak to one another, but that was the extent of our interaction during his freshman year.

When I'd see him at the Alphas' informal mixers and meetings, he'd tried to engage me in conversation, and although I was polite, I didn't think Aaron was "Alpha material." Didn't think he could hack it, so I really didn't take him seriously. Don't get me wrong—he was a real smart guy and had graduated high school a year early. He certainly looked the part. I guess I had this picture of what an Alpha should be and what my line brothers should look and be like, and well, Aaron just didn't fit the profile.

Once we officially went on line (a term used to describe pledging activities), we would meet every night and then come to my apartment, which was where all the neophytes were supposed to spend the night. Almost every night all my line brothers would leave to do their own thing, leaving me with all the work. But not Aaron. He'd strike up a conversation and just hang around.

I finally realized he wasn't going anywhere, so I just started talking to him. Soon, four hours had passed. We found out we had many of the same interests, goals, and dreams for our lives after graduation.

Ironically, early in our pledge process some of us had gathered and discussed who we needed to look out for and who we thought might be the weak link. We all had agreed that Aaron might need a little help. In a weird twist of irony, he turned out to be the most level-headed and stable of us all. We thought we needed to look out for him, when we ended up being the ones breaking down.

It's funny how life works out sometimes. Not only is Aaron one of my closest friends today, but he's also a creative genius. When I started my first business, he designed my website, logo, business cards, and traveled to every show I did and never asked for one single dime. When I launched the Texas Black Expo, he created our website, all our flyers, and other marketing for the first three years, while working a full-time job.

He's the most giving person I know, and without him I can't even imagine how I could have made it in business. Anytime I'm in a crunch and need advice, he's the first person I call. Whether it's technical help, business strategy, or government and politics, I can count on him to have an interesting perspective that challenges me and keeps me grounded.

That's the power of relationships. Sometimes the best ones start in the most unlikely places, under the most unlikely circumstances. We all have preconceived perceptions and beliefs of what we think people should be, do, and say. What folks rarely realize is that most of the time we want people to do and say the things most closely aligned with our own beliefs so that we can say, "Look at me! I'm smart! Everybody thinks like I do."

But what actually makes the world so interesting is that everybody is different, everybody is unique, and everybody brings substantial value to relationships. Sometimes I think about how close I came to missing out on a great friendship with Aaron, all because I looked at him and thought, "He doesn't have what it takes to hang with guys like me."

Turns out Aaron actually taught me a valuable leadership lesson: If you don't dismiss your natural tendency to judge people by what you think you see in them and instead get to know people, you'll potentially miss out on the opportunity to connect with someone who can enrich your life or company in unimaginable ways.

PART I TAKEAWAYS

- You can't lead them if you don't love them.

- Great leaders get to know people and value what makes them unique.

- They won't follow you if they don't believe you respect them, understand them, and can help them get what they want.

- Leadership's not about getting people to do what you want them to do.

- Succeeding in business is as much about creating good relationships as it is about the numbers and data.

- The stronger your relationship with those following you, the stronger their desire to help you succeed.

- People are wired to want what they want for their lives—not what you want for their lives.

- Leadership is a contact sport. If you're not ready to work, keep it moving.

- Law of Respect: Everyone wants respect, and no one wants to be disrespected or disrespectful.

PART II:
CONFLICT
RESOLUTION

"The thing is, you cannot ask people to coexist by having one side bow their heads and rely on a solution that is only good for the other side. What you can do is stop blaming each other and engage in dialogue with one person at a time."

~Izzeldin Abuelaish

EXPO—SING MY WEAKNESSES

We all have leadership blind spots.

Back in 2007, my company, Texas Black Expo, Inc., hosted its fourth annual Houston Black Expo, which is the largest African American trade show in Texas. While our organization has been very successful, we don't have a large staff. As a matter of fact, I am the staff. Although at the actual Expo we may have three to four staff members and another 50 volunteers, during the rest of the year, it's pretty much just me. Lots of folks in Houston know or know of Jerome Love. They know I'm the one to come to if there's a problem at the Expo.

Each year at the event we have a number of stages that feature different types of activities, from home-buying workshops to comedy shows. This particular year we had a presentation scheduled at 3 p.m. by the Jamaica Travel Authority to talk about the benefits of Jamaica.

Their presentation was to take place on what we call the seminar stage, which was the smallest of all the stages with fewer amenities. In fact, on the seminar stage there's only a podium microphone unless the presenter makes other arrangements to have additional audio / visual equipment.

Around 2:45 mayhem broke out at the Expo. At the same time Jamaica Tourist Authority was to present, a well-known cosmetic surgeon was also set to present on various types of procedures. His presentation was to include a number of before and after shots, which one of my staff members felt were inappropriate at a family show.

They'd told me to review his pictures and make the call. Additionally, there was an exhibitor who demanded a refund, alleging that some of his items had been stolen. As if those problems weren't enough, the city health inspector made a surprise visit and threatened to shut the show down because the cleaning station on the cooking stage hadn't been changed. I was dealing with a lot, as you can see.

In the midst of all these minor emergencies, a frantic representative from the Jamaica Tourist Authority ran up to me and said, "Jerome, it's 2:45 and our screen and projector aren't set up on the seminar stage."

My first thought was, "I already know the seminar stage projector isn't set up because it doesn't come with a projector!" I didn't actually say those words, but that's what I thought.

I turned to him and said rather curtly, "The seminar stage doesn't come with a projector and screen." And with that I proceeded to take care of another matter that I thought was more pressing.

About a week or so after the Expo, I typically reach out to vendors and sponsors to thank them for their support. I know I could never do the Expo without them, and I want them to know how much I appreciated their support.

So I was going through my calls, talking to vendors who were giving me great feedback for making the event better. I was feeling pretty good about myself and the business until I made the last call of the day. Nothing really could've prepared me for my call with the Jamaica Travel Authority.

"How was your experience at the Houston Black Expo?" I asked enthusiastically.

The young lady responded emphatically, "It was terrible!" I was shocked.

Honestly at that point, I didn't even recall the situation at the Expo, so my response was simply, "Really? What happened?"

"We didn't appreciate the way you treated us. Our presentation was delayed due to not having our projection screen, and my director said you just blew him off and he felt insulted."

Her words hit me like a ton of cement.

At that point the whole situation came back to me, and what could I say? Nothing really. I apologized, but the reality was the damage had been done, and they haven't returned to the Expo since 2007.

I wish I could say they haven't returned because the Expo didn't deliver the business outcomes they hoped for. Instead I had to face the fact that their decision not to return was purely relational. In fact, it was completely my fault. Again, I'd been an inept leader and dismal at resolving conflict.

Had I taken a moment to listen, I would have found that they *had* actually ordered a projection screen prior to the Expo. In fact, the screen was in a box right next to the stage, and the audio / visual guys were just waiting for someone to tell them where to put it. But again, I assumed I knew what was going on and failed to listen.

Ever felt like the Jamaica Tourist Authority? All you want is a little TLC, but the person in charge is so busy being a big shot they don't realize they're about to lose your business? Or maybe you were me in the scenario. You're juggling a thousand things and being pulled in 12 different directions. And instead of appointing someone to take care of customers, you try to be all things to all people, and you end up damaging your brand.

I learned many lessons as a result of this goof-up, but the biggest one was to hire people to do the things you're not great at. I should've had someone who was great with people taking care of our vendors, making sure they felt like royalty. Had I put my customers first and been better at resolving conflict, perhaps the Jamaica Tourist Authority would still be a satisfied customer.

I start this section with that story because it illustrates the many, many ways we derail our own success. Sometimes we're completely unaware of our own behaviors. We have no one around us who will give us perspective to help us because most supposed leaders don't really listen to anyone else. Why? Because some of us think we always know better. This all-knowing arrogance is actually the killer of conflict resolution. So let's get started helping you become a better leader during conflict.

What exactly IS Conflict?

Conflict is the tension that makes the clock work. It's the X-factor in blockbuster movies. It's the cherry on top of the sundae in sports when a Cinderella team is trying to beat Goliath. We'd all agree that a movie without conflict would be pretty useless. We'd all probably agree that if the sports teams that should win all the time actually won all the time, sports wouldn't be worth all the beer and chips we eat during them. Yet while we universally agree on the previous two points, we've somehow convinced ourselves that conflict in the workplace or in personal relationships is a bad thing, a very bad thing.you look at archived videos of him interacting with people, you'll see how well he connects on a simple human level with everyone he encounters.

Conflict is not only a natural part of human relationships, but it's also necessary for growth and success. If we all agreed on everything, that would be a pretty boring existence. The trick is not to avoid conflict but to use it to achieve goals. Use it to enhance relationships. Leverage it to obliterate your team's previous numbers.

Think about all the ways we've been conditioned to avoid conflict.

When a baby doesn't cry, we say, "Oh, he's such a good baby; he never cries."

When someone disagrees in the business meeting, we call that individual "confrontational."

When a spouse expresses displeasure with something the other spouse has done, the accused spouse asks, "Why are you so difficult?"

And the beat goes on. We love to hate conflict and I want to change that. A good relationship is not characterized by the lack of conflict. When people are honest, there will naturally be conflict. We're all different. We all have different natures and nurtures, so conflict is to be expected. The true determining factor of the success of a relationship is the parties' ability to resolve and leverage the conflict.

Conflict is not always the result of a misunderstanding. That's a misnomer.

Conflict is the result of one fundamental truth: We are individuals, we are human, and we are different. No two people, no matter how similar they believe they are, are that similar. There will be a difference of perspective and opinion—and contrary to popular belief, this is actually good, not bad. It's healthy, not unhealthy.

Everyone's entitled to their opinion. The goal shouldn't be to get someone to agree with you. If you're a leader, it's your job to bring their differences to the table and leverage those differences to move the team or the relationship forward. That's the hard part. That's what *Love Them and Lead Them* is all about.

TWO COMMON COMMUNICATION MODELS

Now that we've established a baseline for what conflict is, it's time to discuss what I believe are the two most common ways people communicate around conflict: productive or condemning. Before we get to the models, I think we can all agree that to be a successful leader, you must have the ability to connect with people. You will never be able to connect with people if they're not open to you. If they have a mental block because they perceive that you don't care about them, it will prevent them from opening up to you, which will prevent you from effectively leading them in or out of conflict.

I'm blessed to have four small children ranging in age from four to nine. One of the first things we did in 2003 when my first daughter was born was to safety-proof the home. We bought all kinds of stuff, including the plastic covers for electrical outlets, which you put into the outlets to prevent kids from sticking foreign objects into them. In addition, if you don't remove the cover, it will also prevent you from plugging in necessary items.

You can't plug in a vacuum, a lamp, a smartphone charger, anything at all. Until you remove the filter, you can't connect. The filter will block your ability to connect. Well, just as those little plastic covers can block your electric connection, people have automatic protectors too. They tend to appear when they feel like they're being accused or judged. Their protectors appear if they don't trust you or if they dislike you.

LOVE'S LAW OF LEADERSHIP

Law of Attack

If a person is attacked, they will defend themselves.

Here's a quick scenario.

John and Sarah are a happily married couple. John comes home and Sarah asks him to take out the trash. John says, "Yeah okay, I'll do it later," then proceeds to the living room to catch some Sportscenter highlights.

Well, you know what happens next, right?

John falls asleep on the couch, wakes up the next day running late for work, so he darts out the door without taking out the trash. When he comes home, he encounters an angry Sarah who says, "The trash men came today. Why didn't you take out the trash? You never do anything around the house."

She verbally attacks him. Sound familiar, guys?

Some men, not all (I hope), would respond the way John did.

"Cut me some slack, will ya? I've been working hard all day to pay these bills, and you have the audacity to say I don't help. I took the trash out the last three times, not to mention I cut the grass and changed the oil in the car!"

This scenario is doomed form the start as Sarah violated the Law of Attack, which states if a person is attacked, they will defend themselves. And when people are defensive, productivity comes to a screeching halt.

You see, John felt attacked (and probably unappreciated), so he defended himself. His protector automatically appeared. Now, the essence of what these two are arguing about is who is wrong and who is right, but the reality is it really doesn't matter. It started with the task at hand, taking out the trash. Now it's become about how each of them feels and who's right, which are not "chore" issues but rather relationship issues. Unfortunately, in many relationships the focus tends to steer toward making the other person wrong and not about understanding what that individual's feeling.

One thing I always say in my leadership workshops is a simple mantra: It does not matter what is real . . . it only matters what a person feels. Remember that!

Although it was a simple marriage example, it can be applied to multiple situations. This is almost identical to most gung ho, take-charge leaders and those following them. The only difference is when you say, "Why didn't you take out the trash. You never do anything around the house," as Sarah did, a boss might say, "We can't have you always missing deadlines."

You've just verbally assaulted your employee. Not only are they likely to defend themselves, but they'll also automatically shut down to your leadership. And worse, they'll become committed to one thing: proving you wrong!

They don't have the relationship with you that John has with Sarah. So while John's attack on Sarah was overt, an employee's attack is more covert. Most won't attack you verbally, especially if their paycheck depends on it. Instead, they may launch a covert attack by simply blocking you in their minds, undermining your leadership with teammates, and possibly even sending anonymous notes about you to your uppers.

Remember the outlet protector? Once the outlet is blocked, you no longer have the ability to connect.

To minimize this experience with your group or organization, we really need to examine what happens in these situations in order to avoid these pitfalls in the future. It's imperative that you get a firm grasp on what I call the relationship or communication paradigm; this is where these two communication approaches come into play.

COMMUNICATION PARADIGM

During conflict, leaders typically revert to two kinds of communication: condemnation or productivity. They each render distinctly different results.

Condemnation

Your dictionary will define "condemnation" as the act of declaring something awful, evil, or wrong. Simply put, condemnation is primarily focused on an assessment or judgment of the individual, with little or no concern for the overall goal of the relationship.

Utilizing the example above, let's break it down further. When Sarah attacks John, she's operating from her emotional wheelhouse of feeling unsupported by her husband. In other words, her words reveal that perhaps she feels she carries a heavy load at home and that John is not pulling his weight.

Cut to John, who feels he's unappreciated for his contributions away from home—at work. Neither of them says they feel unappreciated. That would likely feel too vulnerable for them. So they do what most of us do: They direct their insecurities, their hurt or disappointment, at the other person.

Now, how different do you think the interaction would have been had Sarah said something along these lines: "Honey, I really appreciate how hard you work and I know that when you get home, all you wanna do is play your Madden or watch Sportscenter. Would you mind grabbing the trash cans and putting them on the street—the trash guys are coming tomorrow?" Then, follow that up with a big kiss.

What Sarah potentially wants is to avoid having smelly garbage in their garage. She may want not to be faced with an overflowing trash can for the following week—all reasonable things to desire.

What John potentially wants is to be acknowledged for his contributions before he's accused of not being helpful. When he doesn't get what he wants, he strikes back with what he knows will get his point across. But do his words get him closer to the recognition he secretly desires? Absolutely not.

So now you've got two folks who love each other, who are condemning each other rather than supporting each other.

When openness is not modeled by leaders in a business or personal relationship, the result is often very unproductive. Instead of creating a more productive environment of honesty and accountability, many organizations resort to shame, blame, guilt, and verbal assaults.

Productivity

In contrast with the condemnation approach that's rooted in misdirected emotions, the productivity model is solely focused on one thing: results. Whatever is necessary to accomplish the task, that's what you do!

A good leader understands this. They are results-driven people who ALSO love people. They are able to manage their emotions and focus on the task at hand.

Let's take the John and Sarah scenario from earlier.

Leadership is often about forecasting the weather. It's about showing both parties in the relationship how they can contribute to a better existence together—even when the other party isn't their best. Here's what I mean.

Let's say Sarah did exactly as she did in the original scenario. She verbally attacks John for not taking out the trash. Even though Sarah wasn't her best in this situation, this doesn't mean John can't be his best. You see, sometimes, we feel justified in our responses to people, but leaders understand that even though you might be justified in being a jerk, that doesn't mean that behavior serves the team or relationship best. Make sense?

So, even though Sarah attacked John, he still had an opportunity to show up better than he did. He could have responded with openness, saying, "Sorry, Honey, I dropped the ball this time. I'll be better. Can you do me a favor and put a note on the fridge on the day the trash cans need to go out?"

Now, some of you are still in "attack" mode. You're thinking, "John needs to get Sarah straightened out!" But what would that really accomplish in the moment? It might make John feel triumphant, but it doesn't get the results needed in the moment: getting the trash out before the trash men come! Now, to extend John's leadership, I do believe later that night when things have settled down a bit, he should give his wife some insights on communicating with him in a way that will continue to get the results she desires.

What this example reveals is that everybody has a leadership role in relationships. That's a concept that's lost on most people, yet when you get consensus that everyone's a leader, your organization, team, and relationship will flourish in ways you've never imagined.

WHEN CONFLICT BECOMES UNHEALTHY

I have an aunt who remained in a physically abusive relationship for many years. After leaving the relationship, she became an advocate against domestic violence. One day we were talking about why so many women stay in abusive relationships so long.

One of the things I learned in this conversation was the power of perception. In many cases these women would say things like, "My husband is a great person; he's just going through a stressful time in his life," or "He doesn't mean to do it; he's just under a lot of pressure right now."

As dysfunctional as this may sound to some of you, this is a clear illustration of the power of perception. Now, I'm no domestic violence expert, but it was difficult for me to understand how some women still held positive perceptions of men who repeatedly beat them. It just didn't compute for me.

My aunt explained that domestic violence is not as black and white as I might have wanted to believe. She shared the role that shame and fantasy play in keeping women in bad relationships—not to mention the progressively fearful environment that's nurtured the longer she stays.

Most women, especially outwardly successful ones, are embarrassed to tell folks they're in an abusive relationship because they're afraid of the backlash from their friends and family. Others maintain a fantasy about what "was" in their relationships or "what can be" once the guy is not under so much pressure. And finally, many batterers begin to threaten women, their children, and their families—which keeps many of them in the relationship. It's complicated, I learned.

I was starting to come to grips with the many dynamics in abusive relationships. Just as people can choose to see good when it's clearly bad, people can also choose to see bad when there is nothing present but good. My wife has helped bring this concept to life for me. She's a very attractive woman—a former model with a lot of the external qualities our society defines as beauty: tall, caramel complexion, long hair, slim waist, cute in the face—the total package. But the most amazing thing is that she's just as beautiful inside.

She is the most selfless person I know, someone who's always trying to help others. With that type of personality, you'd think people would flock to her. Instead, she's shared stories of people who were very mean to her because of her generosity of spirit. Some might call those folks "haters."

When you're successful, when you're a leader making a difference, you're going to attract haters. The conflict that comes with haters is often layered in insecurity and jealousy. People will reject your brilliance not because you're not brilliant but because they're envious of your skills or "package."

As a leader, you may not always be liked. In fact, it's a sure bet you won't be the most popular person in every given situation. On your teams you may have detractors who want you to fail, and who will do everything in their power to make sure you do. When presented with this kind of conflict, you'll need skills in place that prevent this kind of "unproductive" conflict from stalling your team's progress.

UNPRODUCTIVE VS. PRODUCTIVE CONFLICT

As I mentioned, if your thought is to avoid conflict, you're not really cut out for leadership roles. Leaders don't run from conflict; they value it. They see the opportunities inherent in it.

Productive Conflict means that you and your team keep the goal in front of you and that you're committed to hearing all sides of the situation even if you disagree with it. Unproductive Conflict happens when you (the leader) allow, or your team allows individuals who have no commitment to the team's goals or progress to run your team into the ground with their negativity.

For example, let's say, in Monday's team meeting you throw out an idea to create a new product. You blueprint the product on the whiteboard and ask your team to chime in with their thoughts. Three folks give you their feedback, offering interesting insights to the process. But there's this one individual who doesn't say anything. You ask them what they think and finally they say, "I don't like it."

That's it. That's all they say.

You probe a bit further. "What exactly don't you like about it?"

"I just don't like it. It's stupid."

Now, this is unproductive conflict not because the individual doesn't like your idea but because they won't expound on the specifics of what they dislike. This kind of response does nothing to advance the conversation or your team. Of course, the goal isn't to get everyone to agree; the goal is to get everyone to participate. An individual who blatantly attempts to derail progress is not an active contributor to the team's goals.

Conflict Imprints

A good leader is charged with understanding that most folks never overcome the clunky conflict resolution skills most of us endure with the folks who raised us. In other words, the imprints of how our parents handled conflict are often transferred over into our adult relationships unless we undo them. For example, if you grew up with parents who yelled and screamed at each other when they disagreed, you're likely to (a) yell and scream when you disagree because it's familiar and you thrive in that environment, or (b) avoid yelling and screaming because it's familiar but you want to avoid that environment.

As a leader on a team of 12, you must realize that you may have 12 different conflict resolution models on your team! How do you handle that? Let's break down 10 truths leaders must be aware of prior to conflict in order to be able to lead through it.

TRUTH #1: MOST PEOPLE FEAR AND WANT TO AVOID CONFLICT.

I don't care what you believe; most of us are terrified of conflict. Why? Because we've been conditioned to think it's bad. Bad things happen when we don't agree. Nothing could be further from the truth. Bad things may happen when we don't know how to handle our disagreements in a healthy fashion, but bad things don't happen just because we disagree.

Conflict is nothing more than difference. So how can we, on one hand, rave about embracing diversity in this country and at the same time be so afraid of diversity? So the first thing you must acknowledge as a leader is that we like to work with people who are more like us than unlike us. I'm not saying this is good or bad; I'm saying if we're honest, most of us would agree with that statement.

However, that philosophy will kill your team. Cultures that embrace different ways of thinking in their organizations are more successful. Organizations that aren't afraid to do things a little bit differently tend to be among the world's best innovators.

You, the leader, must set the tone for how conflict and differences will be embraced within your team early and **often.** You can't wait until something happens to try to announce how the team handles conflict. You must lead the way.

LIGHT BULB ACTION STEPS ON TRUTH #1

_____

_____

_____

_____

_____

TRUTH #2: CONFLICT IS OFTEN NOT JUST A DISAGREEMENT ON OPINIONS, PERSPECTIVES, OR VALUES. IT'S A MIRROR THAT WE'RE ALIVE, HUMAN, AND DIFFERENT.

When there's conflict on your team, be the first on the scene to encourage what's underneath the conflict: passion, differences, and commitment to be the best. Get excited about it and watch how your team responds. They may think you're crazy for a moment, but then they'll appreciate the innovative approach to it. Think about it. When you, the leader, frame conflict differently, the people embroiled in the conflict will approach resolving it differently.

LIGHT BULB ACTION STEPS ON TRUTH #2

_____

_____

_____

_____

_____

TRUTH #3: CONFLICTS THAT START OUT AS MINOR CUTS GROW INTO INFECTIONS IF IGNORED.

It's important to get to the heart of the conflict within hours of it surfacing. For instance, if you've internalized a colleague's or friend's behavior in a certain way, it's best to ask them about it sooner than later. Don't just assume you've nailed it.

I've seen too many instances where you think one thing happened, and your friend thinks one thing happened. You both act upon your "perceptions" of what happened, and the relationship or partnership suffers because neither of you reached out to gain consensus. Happens all the time.

When you're in a leadership role, you must constantly be on the "prowl" for things that might prevent your team from optimal levels of performance, as well as behaviors that are helping to optimize performance and results.

LIGHT BULB ACTION STEPS ON TRUTH #3

_____

_____

_____

_____

_____

TRUTH #4: CONFLICT WILL NOT RESOLVE ITSELF.

Some leaders seem to think, "If I just 'let it be, it'll take care of itself." Name one instance where that's actually happened. You can't. Even if you never heard a peep about the conflict, it didn't really resolve itself. Don't fool yourself. The worst thing you can do as a leader is to allow conflict to "work itself out." That attitude may come back to bite you at the worst time possible.

Now, I'm not recommending that you make everything a big deal, but I am suggesting that you not be afraid to get your hands dirty if it means an opportunity for your team to grow and get better as a result.

LIGHT BULB ACTION STEPS ON TRUTH #4

_____

_____

_____

_____

_____

TRUTH #5: MOST FOLKS' INITIAL RESPONSE TO CONFLICT IS A SELFISH ONE.

Our natural propensity to allow our innate survival instincts to guide our actions explains why we respond selfishly when there's conflict. That's why it's important in business to keep the team in view. In personal relationships you keep the bigger picture—the marriage, the kids—in the forefront. When our sense of safety or success is threatened, we go to our corners.

Great leaders resist the temptation to put on boxing gloves with their teams. Instead, they put on a whistle so that they can moderate the conflict in a way that results in a winning decision for the team—not for any one individual.

LIGHT BULB ACTION STEPS ON TRUTH #5

_____

_____

_____

_____

_____

TRUTH #6: CONFLICT IGNITES UNBELIEVABLE EMOTIONS. YOU MUST BE PREPARED FOR THE RANGE OF EMOTIONS THAT SHOW UP WHEN CONFLICT ARISES.

Many folks are of the opinion that men don't show enough emotions and that women show too many emotions. Actually, what we're really saying is men don't show the emotions women show and vice versa. Let me explain. Men are very emotional. You can see it when they're threatened or passionate about something.

I'm a fan of the show *Celebrity Apprentice*. It's a reality show that pits celebrities against celebrities in competitions to raise money for charities. It has a 13-episode season, and during the course of the show, you'll see some of the most competitive people on the planet. The men yell and order people around. They hoot and holler when they succeed and sulk when they don't. If their team wins, they bump chests and high five like they've just won an NCAA championship. Emotional, right?

The women exhibit some of the same behaviors. They show their competence through the challenges. They're demanding and they don't back down. When they win, they're exuberant and joyful. The main difference? When things don't go their way, sometimes they cry.

Now, there's nothing wrong with crying, but I find it kind of curious that the producers of *Celebrity Apprentice* choose to portray women as catty criers. The viewers are left with the perception that women are emotional, and men are not. The reality is that both genders exhibit a range of emotions when stakes rise. Network producers simply choose to paint a picture that feeds into common gender stereotypes.

Do you do this? As a leader, are you feeding into common stereotypes when conflict arises? Are those stereotypes stopping you from being an effective leader?

LIGHT BULB ACTION STEPS ON TRUTH #6

_____

_____

_____

_____

_____

TRUTH #7: CONFLICT PRESENTS AN OPPORTUNITY FOR
GROWTH AND NEW LEVELS OF SUCCESS.

When you're able to deal with conflict in a relationship in a productive way, it builds trust. You can feel secure knowing your relationship can survive challenges and disagreements. In a business or personal relationship, trust is vital to success. Yet many CEOs underestimate the importance of their conflict resolution skills in the development of a trust-centered organization. Fortunately, you won't make that mistake after reading this book.

The truth is when you start to value healthy conflict resolution, so will the rest of your team. So, yes, like everything else I'm saying in this book, you need to first look in the mirror, do your own work around conflict, and then model healthy conflict resolution behavior.

LIGHT BULB ACTION STEPS ON TRUTH #7

_____

_____

_____

_____

_____

TRUTH #8: YOU MUST CHANGE THE CULTURE OF "WIN-LOSS" IN CONFLICT.

The winner has to be whatever's best for the relationship or team—not the individuals in the matter. This is where the rubber starts to meet the road. Too many would-be-great leaders fail on this point. Most people go into a conflict thinking if they "give in," they lose. Others enter the resolution process thinking they must win at all cost. Healthy organizations don't operate this way, which means leaders of unhealthy organizations must change the conversations around conflict so that it's no longer a win-loss environment when it comes to this critical growth topic.

Leaders in unhealthy organizations typically can't separate their "feelings" about the individuals involved in the matter from what really matters—what's best for the team, family, or relationship.

This is also where many leaders lose the respect of their team. If players on a team see that you don't have the discipline to discern the best course for the team, you will lose them. And getting them back will be one major uphill battle.

LIGHT BULB ACTION STEPS ON TRUTH #8

_____

_____

_____

TRUTH #9: MOST PEOPLE ARE NOT CONFIDENT IN CONFLICT
BECAUSE THEY FEEL THREATENED.

This is a very important truth. Think about the way you feel when you hear your significant other say the dreaded four words: We have to talk. No man likes hearing that phrase! I suspect women feel the same way, but I can speak only from a male perspective. When my wife says, "Baby, we need to talk," I usually think to myself, "Aw, man, here we go," or "What did I do now?"

My kids probably feel the same way when I say, "Let's have a family meeting." They know it's probably gonna have something to do with chores or behavior. That's just the nature of conflict. Most of us don't greet it with a smile. But why is that?

Well, it's because we automatically feel threatened. Something we care about or value is threatened by conflict—at least that's how most of us view it. So if my wife says we need to talk, what's potentially threatened is our peace, our calm environment. Now, of course I'm wrong, and all she wants to do is talk about our plans for the weekend or what we're gonna eat for dinner.

What kinds of conflict disrupt an organization? How about when a bigwig comes to town unexpectedly? The whispers start circulating. "Mr. X is in town. Are they laying us off?" Or if the leader of the company calls an impromptu meeting, most folks enter the conference room with blank faces, praying they didn't screw something up, right?

In those famed Performance Review sessions, ever notice that the person being reviewed never smiles? Great leaders help their followers approach even tough situations differently. If you've done a good job of cultivating an environment that doesn't shy away from conflict but instead welcomes it with heart, dignity, and openness, your followers will reward the company with loyalty and dedication.

LIGHT BULB ACTION STEPS ON TRUTH #9

_____

_____

_____

_____

_____

TRUTH 10: YOUR TEAM HAS WATCHED YOU HANDLE CONFLICT.

They either feel safe or fearful because of your leadership style—they've seen you operate.

Do not get it twisted. Your employees, family, friends, and followers have your number. They've been watching and they've taken copious notes. If you've been a bad leader, especially in the conflict category, you won't be able to rally your troops. I'm not saying they won't follow you; I'm saying they won't run through a cement wall for you.

I played youth sports, and there were always those coaches we kids couldn't wait to follow. There were also those coaches we tuned out for lots of different reasons.

Sometimes they didn't quite walk their talk. Other times we just didn't feel the coach had our best interests at heart. But there was that one coach that we knew had no hidden agenda. That coach that held us all to the same standard. That guy got us to do things the others couldn't have gotten us to do if they'd paid us.

It's the same with you and those under your leadership. They're watching you. They're depending on you to step up to the plate and handle the tough situations fairly. To communicate the team's vision. To have their backs. To be a role model for healthy conflict resolution.

LIGHT BULB ACTION STEPS ON TRUTH #10

_____

_____

_____

_____

_____

Unproductive Conflict Resolution	Productive Conflict Resolution
Talking over the other person and refusing to listen to their experience	Affirming that you hear the other side of the conflict
Exploding, yelling, and name-calling	Non-defensive responses that indicate you are not dismissing everything they say
Silence, withdrawal, or alienation	Staying engaged in the conversation even if it's hard
Avoiding and not acknowledging that something's wrong	Initiating the conversation with the belief that things can be resolved

LEADERSHIP VS. DOMINANCE

Along my leadership journey I've tried to impose my will with no concern for others. I was a dominator who was totally oblivious to those under my tutelage. Somehow I started to notice how people were responding to me, and I began to overcompensate. Even if I had a strong opinion on something, I began to bite my tongue and just try to float along in order not to offend others. Then I became frustrated because that approach didn't feel right either.

I began to realize that good leadership is no more about dominating each and every situation than it is about giving in in order to be liked. There has to be a balance. What happens in one situation with one person may not be applicable in another situation with another person.

I have four children, and I quickly learned what works for one doesn't necessarily work for another. This led me to develop what I call a S.T.O.P. Analysis when conflict arises.

"S.T.O.P." stands for:

S = Significance

T = Timing

O = Outcome

P = Pattern

Prior to engaging in any type of confrontation or conflict, it's imperative that you go through this assessment.

S – Significance

Before you decide to confront that employee or team

member or whoever it is you had the privilege of leading, ask yourself: What is that person's significance? What role do they play in the overall success of the team or organization? The answer to this question will determine if, how, and when you opt to address this person. How will the possible loss of this person positively or negatively affect the overall goal your organization is trying to accomplish? And is that goal worth possibly destroying the culture? Is there a way to approach the individual that won't absolutely destroy everything you and your team have built?

In his book under the same title, Daniel Goleman discusses what's called Emotional Intelligence. He delineates the five crucial skills of emotional intelligence and shows how they determine our success in relationships, work, and even our physical well-being. What emerges from his report is a fresh, new conversation about being smart. His work shows that your ability to relate may be as important as your mental capacity to figure things out, a skill that's highly valued in our society. Emotional intelligence isn't a score but a range of the five following skills.

Self-awareness: Knowing what you're feeling and using that self-awareness as a guide

Managing emotions: Do you fall apart under stress?

Motivation: Can you keep working toward your goals?

Empathy: Knowing how people feel without them telling you with words

Social skills: How well you function in relationships

Let's say you're working on a job you hate and every day you dream of telling your boss off. If this is your dream or desire, why don't you just march right in there and tell them off? The reason is emotional intelligence, hopefully.

You know you need the job. You know that if you lose your income, you and your family will suffer, right? So when your boss gets on your last nerve, are you going to "keep it real" or smile and take it? You don't choose to swallow your pride because you're weak; you swallow your pride because you're smart—emotionally.

I used to watch the Dave Chappelle show. One time I saw a segment entitled, "When Keeping It Real Goes Wrong." In this segment it showed a guy, let's call him Jim, at a party with his girlfriend and another guy tries to hit on her. They then paused the screen and talked about his options.

Option #1 was to brush it off and act like it didn't happen, which represents emotional intelligence.

Option #2 was to "Keep it Real" and confront the guy.

They then showed the outcomes of each. With Option #1 he put aside his ego and pride and moved on. The end result? He and his girl go on to get married, have kids, and have a successful life.

With Option #2 he chose to confront the guy. What he didn't know was the guy was a black belt in karate. The guy proceeded to beat him until he was unconscious. He was hospitalized for a few weeks, and he never regained full functionality of his body. His girlfriend dumped him and married his best friend. Jim lived with his mom for the rest of his life. Why? Because he showed no emotional intelligence at the club. He didn't recognize the significance of the moment.

Now, of course this is an extreme example, but hopefully you get my point. Don't simply do things based on your emotions. Assess the situation. Consider the potential outcome, and then either choose to withdraw or to engage.

Let's say one of your employees is not a morning person but you are. You walk into the office and get ready to ask her why she's looking like somebody stole her puppy. But before you address her about her lethargy, you ask yourself: What is her significance? Is she the number one salesperson on your team? And even if she's not, she has every right not to be a morning person and not feel judged for it. Leadership isn't about making your team clones of each other. It's about bringing out the best in all of them.

T – Timing

Timing is everything. The right action at the wrong time will typically yield the wrong result every time. The wrong action at the right time could yield the wrong result. Everything does not have to be addressed when it happens. Sometimes letting the situation breathe a little is the best medicine.

In college I served as second vice president of my fraternity. Though there were a number or tasks assigned to me, the primary role was to coordinate the parties, our number one fundraisers.

In order to successfully coordinate a party, I had a team of people I had to lead in producing a successful event. My role was to locate the venue, negotiate the terms, and ensure payment was made. Aaron's primary role was to create the flyers for the party, so he was the technical guy. Rodney's job was promotions and manning the door. He would go down to 6th street in Austin, or wherever other parties were going to be, and recruit.

My personality profile was high Choleric, the aggressive, insensitive one that had a knack for getting things done. Aaron was more Melancholy, the black-and-white guy who loved numbers and data. Rodney, on the other hand, was an off-the-charts Phlegmatic. That's the people person, always cracking jokes, knows where the best party will be—the guy folks liked being around. However, the Phlegmatics are not your best organizers. They can be a bit flaky at times. Punctuality is not normally their priority. You can imagine that Rodney and I clashed on occasion.

When having a party, the rule was to show up an hour ahead of time. But Rodney would always be late. Not only would he be late, but it didn't seem to matter to him. He'd stroll in smiling, making jokes as if he'd arrived on time. This drove me nuts.

One time before our Texas Relays event, which was our biggest party of the year, I'd had enough. The party started at 10 o'clock at night. He showed up at 9:36 wearing a big grin. I lit into him. "Where have you been? This doesn't make any sense!"

My words carried the harshness and the weight of all the times he'd been late. I was fed up and I wanted to make sure he knew it. There we were: two enterprising young men with the same goal of putting on a great party, two men with very different approaches to that goal. I continued to berate him—so much so that he left. Right before our biggest fundraiser of the year.

To make matters worse there was a line of about 100 people outside waiting to get into the party. And no one was working the door. I became even more livid. Clearly, my judgment had been impaired. It was not the proper time to address Rodney, even if it was *"right."* In that one quick decision, I'd jeopardized the entire project and 50 percent of our annual revenue. I had not exercised great emotional intelligence.

Fortunately, Aaron was able catch Rodney before he got too far away and calm him down. His diligence allowed us to avoid potential disaster. My lack of leadership almost cost us thousands of dollars.

This is a killer example of how my S.T.O.P. Analysis would have been invaluable to me as a leader. Had I known what I know now, I would have recognized that my timing was atrocious. I would have also known to adjust my approach based on Rodney's importance to our team. I'm not saying I wouldn't have said *anything* to Rodney; I'm saying I would have come at him a little bit differently so that my approach wouldn't potentially wreck our team's success or progress. I learned the hard way that leading is about hard work and teamwork. You need people around you who can compensate for and cover your shortcomings. You have to have an Aaron on your team who can come behind and clean up your mess if you exercise poor judgment.

Now that I think back, I didn't know how to value Aaron or Rodney, yet I needed them both. In fact, we all needed each other, but we didn't know how to appreciate each other. I know some of you may be thinking, "Screw that. I'm the boss or I'm the leader. That's too much work." And you're right. Being an effective, successful leader is work. So put on your helmet and roll up your sleeves. We're just getting started.

O – Outcome

Never lose sight of the end game. Your goal. There'll be plenty of time to revisit the process after you've reached the finish line, but if your leadership crumbles during the race, you may never get there.

Sometimes we're so focused on punishing people that we don't take time to truly evaluate the infraction. Did it negatively impact our ability to reach our goal?

P – Pattern

There are behaviors that contribute to the success of organizations and those that contribute to its demise. Leaders have to possess enough clarity to be able to distinguish between the two. If punctuality is one of the company's core values and one of the employees is perpetually late, costing the company valuable productive time and money, then as a leader, you must address this pattern. You can't just let it slide. Why? Because core values are just that. They are principles by which the company operates with good reason. Failure to consistently adhere to core success values will likely lead to a breakdown in the fabric of what makes the company work. This is, of course, if those values are embraced by the team.

Now, you also have to be able to discern the difference between a one-time mistake and what's becoming a pattern, a recurring offense. You don't want to treat a single instance as though it happens all the time; this'll only inflame the situation.

When Anger Works

I'm not one of those people who believes anger's wrong. I think productive anger has a place in relationships at home and at work. If the store down the street is kicking your store's butt, you should be angry. But not the kind of angry that compels you to start saying bad things about your competitor in the newspaper. Not the kind of angry that drives you to vandalize the store. The kind of anger that motivates you and your team to figure out how you can close the gap between the market share. Now that's productive anger.

The problem with most folks is that most of their anger's unproductive. Completely unproductive. Parents, you know what I'm talking about. Sometimes we get so frustrated with our kids that we say and do things that make no sense at all. If you've had a hard day at work and you walk into the house and your kid's room seems a little messier than normal, you might send them to bed even though it's only 5:45 on a Friday evening. Unproductive anger. Misdirected anger.

This kind of behavior happens in corporations every single day. As a leader you've got to figure out how to help your team channel conflict and anger into productive activities.

THE ANGRY LEADER

If you've watched recent headlines, you've surely seen the fiasco at Rutgers University with now-ex-basketball coach Tim Rice. In a move that probably should have happened six months earlier, he was removed from his position as head basketball coach after administrators viewed videotape of him shouting homophobic slurs, berating, shoving, pushing, screaming, punching, and belittling his players during practices. Apparently, Rice was very angry. About what, no one seems to know. But surely a missed jumpshot or defensive assignment can't be the cause of such behavior.

Clearly, I'm not privy to all the inside scoop at Rutgers University, but I can tell you from seeing videotape of these incidences that Tim Rice was a highly ineffective leader, an inappropriate commander in chief of his basketball program. Sports has long been the domain where aggressive behavior is allowed, almost ignored. If Rice had been the CEO of a company, he would have been fired on the spot after his first offense. But because he leads the attack in a boiler room situation, he was given latitude to behave like a raving maniac.

Clearly Tim Rice was angry. About what, we may never know. But you can't lead effectively if you're angry. You can't take your anger out on your employees. And you can't think you're going to grow an organization or keep your job by displaying unprofessional and demeaning behavior toward others. Rice's unproductive anger cost him his job and brought much embarrassment to his employer, Rutgers University. What's yours costing you?

EFFECTIVE STRESS TOOLS

It's no secret that Americans work longer than most people on the planet. We believe this makes us a better, stronger nation. But does it? Are the long hours taking their toll on us?

Companies like Apple believe longer doesn't always mean better. In fact, companies like Google, Facebook, and Zappos have long understood that to keep your team "humming" like a fine-tuned automobile, you have to help them manage the stressors of a high-performing team.

So I wasn't surprised to hear that many corporations like Zappos were putting in massage rooms and nap rooms on their campuses. They recognize the need to recharge or decompress during a busy work day. And instead of trying to suck every ounce of blood out of their employees, they're taking a different route.

Nap Pods are popping up in corporations across America. Arianna Huffington, whose authority website, *The Huffington Post*, was bought by AOL for $4.2 billion, outfitted their new digs in New York with NapQuest rooms and Energy Pods.

According to a 2008 poll by the National Sleep Foundation, 28 percent of the 1,000 respondents said sleepiness interferes with their daytime activities at least a few days each month.

As people begin to take more non-illness related sick days, companies are getting smarter. They're starting to sing a new song: Let's love them and lead them a little better, and they'll give the company a little more. Guess what? It's working.

The results of making the shift?

Companies that have instituted these kinds of programs are seeing record returns in profits and productivity. All because they weren't afraid to approach business in a different way. All because they used the natural occurrence of stress—which is a form of conflict—to their advantage.

FOUR WAYS YOU CAN HELP DE-STRESS YOUR HOME OR WORKPLACE

De-Stressor #1: Have Mandatory Fun or Themed Days.

I know it sounds like an oxymoron but sometimes ya gotta make people have fun! Something as simple as a costume day or a Way Back Wednesday celebration at lunchtime will get you amazing mileage as a leader. If home or work is always "strictly business," productivity and profits will eventually suffer, trust me.

De-Stressor #2: Break the Ice Before Diving into Business.

Before you start the weekly meeting, have a quick, fun ice-

Is a great cook	Runs at least 3 miles a week	Plays video games every day	Has 5 or more children
Would like to sky dive	Bought a new house this year	Just became an empty nester	Played college football

breaker like Networking Bingo. If you look at the box below, you'll see squares filled with different topics. The goal is to give the folks in the room a chance to get to know the other folks in the room. Teams always find out fun tidbits about their coworkers, friends, and/or family with this game. It's fast, it's fun, and it's an effective icebreaker that allows the leader or whoever's running the meeting to segue right into the business at hand.

How It Works: Each person gets a game card, sorta like a bingo card. You set the timer to five minutes. The goal is to fill in as many squares as possible in the five minutes. You can even have prizes. When time expires, the leader reads every square and asks who fits the square. So if one square reads: "traveled to Europe last year," you'd say, "Who traveled to Europe last year?" Be creative with the information in the square. It's always fun to include things like, "Prefers eating dessert first," or "Has a fitness equipment cemetery in their home or garage."

De-Stressor #3: Offer Yoga Classes.

You can find a teacher in your community who comes in once a week or so and offers a before-work, lunchtime, or after-work yoga class. You'd be surprised how many folks would take you up on the offer to do yoga, especially if you pay for it.

De-Stressor #4: Aromatherapy

Yes, the way your home or office space smells has a lot to do with the level of stress there. Aromas are powerful and can create anxiety and /or calm. Aromatherapy is the use of essential oils (botanical extracts or essences) from flowers, herbs, and trees to care for the body and promote health and well-being. There are literally thousands to choose from, but they include lemon, lavender, and ylang-ylang (to soothe stress and relax), and peppermint and eucalyptus (for mental acuity and extra energy). You can use the actual oils in containers or candles that emit the smell.

COMMUNICATION IS KEY

Have you noticed that most of the concepts and principles of this book revolve around one central theme—better, more effective communication? Communication is central to being a successful leader and developing deeper connections with people (which leads to unbelievable influence).

Something as simple as speaking to a coworker walking down the hall can have a profound impact on the company culture. It validates them. Think about it. Let's say you're in the break room at your office. Your best friend who works in office with you and whom you haven't see all day walks in. She walks to the refrigerator, opens it, grabs a bottled water, and then leaves the room without saying a word. What would you think? Your average individual would immediately think something was wrong. Why? Because, she didn't speak or communicate with you. You'd wonder, "What's wrong with her?" or "I wonder what I did?" Many people might even feel somewhat offended. That's when it's helpful to reference whether you're having a Sanguine or Choleric moment, and how you can turn the moment into a leadership opportunity.

Doing the little things like saying hello or engaging in idle chitchat when you get home from the office can be a challenge for many married couples. Sometimes you just have a lot on your mind. Sometimes you just wanna enjoy the silence. It's not that you don't love your spouse or your mate; you're usually just preoccupied with the work you think you've left at the office. Maybe it's just me. I'm sure you're exemplary spouses, so I won't be too presumptuous and get anyone in trouble out there, so let me just say it's a challenge in my marriage from time to time. Fortunately, I have a wonderful wife who's very patient and understands some of my shortcomings, so it isn't a major problem in our home anymore.

Remember my 3-Step Connection process from earlier?

1. Spark emotion.

2. Make connection.

3. Get down to business.

Raise your hand if you're like me and your natural rhythm is to go straight to Number 3? I know; it saves time and gets to the point, but it does nothing to build connection and trust, two things you must have to grow your influence and leadership profile, which is what *Love Them and Lead Them* is all about.

Now let me share a quick example of how conflict is born in relationships every day and how I was able to learn from past mistakes and leverage my 3-Step Connection process to connect with my wife.

When your baby's born, typically the hospital sends you home with a bag of goodies for the baby. You know, things like diapers, wipes, and blankets. When my son was born, the goody bag also included a new type of pacifier called a *Soothie*. My son loved it. It was almost like a drug addiction. He acted like he couldn't live without it. Matter of fact, it was so bad that he wouldn't take any other type of pacifier! It was hilarious. One day we tried to fool him a couple times and slide one of the other "grocery store" pacifiers into his mouth, and he'd immediately spit it out.

Well, one day, wouldn't you know, he lost it. We attempted to, yes, pacify him with a substitute pacifier, but he rejected them all. And we all know that if you've got an unhappy baby, you've got an unhappy wife and an unhappy home. So I was highly motivated to not only take care of my son and my wife, but also to get some peace myself!

So the next day, after a long day at work, I decided to go to the hospital to get another one. As soon as I got to the nurses' station and started asking about the **Soothie,** they all smiled. They'd seen mothers and probably tons of fathers like me a million times. "It happens all the time," one nurse remarked as she handed me three **Soothie** pacifiers.

It had been a particularly long day at work, and all I could think about driving home was decompressing with my video game. Upon arriving home, I laid the three **Soothies** on the counter and proceeded to the living room to play a game of Madden. My wife walked in, saw the pacifiers, and said, "Oh, you went to the hospital and got more pacifiers?" My left brain, my analytical mind, immediately said silently, "Uh, duh, of course I went to the hospital to get the pacifiers; they're only available at the hospital. Where do you think I got them?"

That's what I *thought*. I didn't actually say what I was thinking. At least not that day. You see, my wife's question wasn't really about the information; she just wanted to talk. She wanted connection. She hadn't seen me all day and she just wanted to talk to me. Even if it meant asking me a question that she already knew the answer to. It wasn't about the topic. It was about the connection. So I responded appropriately and said, "Yeah, babe. Apparently lots of babies can't live without their **Soothie**. The nurses said folks always come in for backups."

We had a short, sweet exchange and that was it. She got what she wanted, and I was a better husband for not being a jerk. Now, I can't say I always do and say the right thing, but on this particularly day I did.

Now, maybe you aren't married. Maybe your communication is with employees, or with a volunteer group, or maybe your child. The situation may change, but there is one constant: Effective, open, heart-centered communication is critical to building and keeping powerful relationships, which allows you to lead more effectively.

EMOTIONAL VS. ANALYTICAL COMMUNICATION

The example I shared about me and my wife happens all the time between the genders. Men are socialized to be more analytical; women are socialized to be more emotional. Neither is wrong or right, but we have to be aware of which is needed in any given situation. Most of the time both are valuable. We need the right brain and left brain sensibilities to navigate through life and business dilemmas.

So there are two aspects of communication we need to explore to ensure you have a thorough understanding of their importance in the discussion on leadership. Those two aspects are emotional and analytical. Depending upon the relationship you have with those following you, this may be the most important aspect of communication. It is certainly imperative in creating the connection that is necessary to become a dynamic leader.

Emotional Communication

My definition of emotional communication is communication that is necessary to maintain, establish, or build a healthy relationship. The pacifier example given above is a sample of this kind of communication. Small talk is rarely just small talk. It may appear to be just dialogue, but it's rarely just dialogue.

We don't do anything without at least one primary and secondary agenda. I'm not saying people are malicious or sneaky; I'm saying it's a natural tendency to have more than one goal when we behave however we behave.

Let's use the "speaking to the coworker" example I mentioned earlier. What could be motivating you to behave this way?

Let's examine ...

- You're courteous.

- You're a decent human being.

- You're a leader.

- You know that people love to feel significant.

- You know that helping someone else feel good will create goodwill.

- You believe that being positive, positively impacts your company.

And so forth and so on.

You see what I mean? Multiple agendas, multiple motivations. One communication can meet so many different needs or send so many different messages.

Remember when you were a kid playing in the sandbox, and your best friend made you mad? What did you do? You gave him the silent treatment. You refused to talk. By not talking you were clearly communicating a message that you were upset, and there was distance in the relationship. This isn't a healthy response, but if we're honest, most of us have given someone in our lives the silent treatment. As a leader, you want to make sure you're not guilty of this inefficient and unproductive communication style, and you want to encourage your followers to foster more open communication as well.

ANALYTICAL COMMUNICATION

Analytical communication, on the other hand, is communication that is needed to relay necessary fact, figures, or details to complete a task. Using the same example of the pacifier, when my wife made the statement, "Oh, you went to the hospital and got more pacifiers?" that was purely emotional. She was simply making conversation. However, if my wife followed up with the question, "Have these pacifiers been sterilized?" then the conversation would have moved from simply emotional to the analytical realm. Now there is critical information that is necessary to ensure our child doesn't put an un-sanitized pacifier in his mouth. While emotional communication may have an analytical aspect, typically there is no emotion in analytical.

Analytical is my natural communication pattern. Analytical is what turned all my fraternity brothers against me and caused people to think I'm uptight. If you're to be a successful leader, you must use both to maximize effectiveness. When my wife and I went through marriage counseling, my pastor told me something that was powerful and relevant to this discussion on communication. He said that for every negative comment you make, you have to counter that with a minimum of 10 positive statements.

In a healthy relationship, you can't expect perfection, and sometimes it's necessary to share a negative or constructive comment so long as it is coming from a productive perspective and not condemnation. This is the only way our relationships can get better. We have a tendency to remember the bad more than we remember the good. So analytical communication in and of itself isn't negative or bad, but after a while it can wear away at the fabric of the relationship. Just be intentional about mixing emotional communication with your analytical to be the best leader you can be.

To that end, in order for you to become a more effective emotional communicator, I've got three power points that can help.

Smile

Smiling creates positive energy. It makes people feel comfortable around you. Let me give you a quick scenario. Let's say you walk into a big department store and need directions to a particular department. You see three different clerks. One is smiling and the others aren't. Which one would you most likely ask for directions?

Smiling gives the appearance of friendliness. People like friendly people. Heck, I probably could have been a lot more effective as a leader in my fraternity had I smiled a bit more. I was so busy being "about the business" that I forgot to be about the business of people. That oversight cost me dearly.

So I challenge you, tomorrow when you walk in your office, smile. When you get home from work, smile. Even if you feel like you have the weight of the world on your shoulders, you don't have to look like it! In addition to making others feel better about you, you'd be amazed at how smiling helps you maintain a positive attitude as well. So try smiling on a consistent basis around your followers; you'll be glad you did.

Eye Contact

Okay, now you're smiling. You now need to practice maintaining eye contact. Look at those you are speaking to directly in the eyes as you talk. Let them know they have your undivided attention. Our society is characterized by massive amounts of pressure. Pressure to be better, faster, more efficient. As a result, we as leaders are trying to juggle 10 different things at once. So when one of our subordinates tries to talk with you, you feel as if you are being bothered. You have more important things to do. Ever talk to a person who was typing away at the computer or, say, moving boxes from one room to the next? It's obvious they are busy, but they are trying to fit you in. Then they say something like, "Go ahead. Keep talking. I'm listening." How do you feel? Probably like you are being an unwanted bother.

Now imagine how you'd feel if your boss was typing away at his computer. You walk in, and he turns from his computer and says, "What's up?" looking you directly in the eyes. Or the person moving the boxes puts the box down, looks you in the eyes, and says, "What do you need?" Now how do you feel? Most likely you feel better about the communication. You feel important. You feel significant because they've stopped work just for you.

Eye contact subconsciously gives the person who is given the attention validation and significance. So the next time your wife or an employee wants to talk, try maintaining eye contact. I'm certain it will tremendously increase your ability to communicate.

Plan For Communication

Who else has 45 things to do by noon tomorrow?

We're all overworked and overextended. As a result of our juggling so many things at once, many times we try to do too much. We try to fit a full day into two hours. This means that many times when we try to communicate or someone tries to communicate with us, there's a breakdown because our mind's in another place. I have an uncle who works for the sheriff's department. As a side job he drives a motorcycle and escorts funeral processions or VIP-type individuals. One day I needed to call him to get some information. When I called, the phone rang, and the conversation went as follows: "Yeah!" my uncle said answering the phone.

"Hey Unc. How you doing?" I responded.

"What you need, boy!" he yelled sharply over the sound of a loud siren.

"Hey, I want to see if I could get your opinion—"

"Ain't got time," he said, cutting me off. "I'm in the middle of an intersection."

"All right," I said as the conversation ended.

My uncle had answered the phone while in the middle of an intersection, on a motorcycle, escorting a funeral. He didn't have time to talk and shouldn't have answered the phone, but he did. As a result, although we briefly spoke, there really wasn't any communication. In my family, insensitive, analytical communication is the order of the day, so I guess you could say my skin is as thick as a cement slab. So I really wasn't offended by my uncle's terse response. However, many folks probably would have felt disrespected.

Though this is a somewhat extreme example, leaders many times find themselves in similar situations—working on several different things when someone calls or an employee knocks on your door. We try to communicate, but we're usually unfocused and short.

In order to alleviate these types of situation, I've learned to plan for better communication. There's a specific time I set aside to return calls and e-mails. I also have a time set aside for all my other daily tasks. So when I need to talk to someone, typically it's on my terms or when I'm prepared for it. This way I can then give them my full attention, and they don't feel as though they're bothering me. It works for me. I believe it'll work for you too.

I know you're busy, but plan a time for communication. Let your employees know when you're available to talk and when you're closed for conversation. Then, during those times when conversation truly is limited, when you're in the middle of something else, at least remember to smile and maintain eye contact.

Finally, remember that emotional communication is most needed in maintaining a relationship, while analytical is vital to accomplishing the task.

WHO'S RIGHT?

In this section I've shared multiple communication examples revealing the need to approach conflict resolution with confidence and an open mind. Whether you're at home or at work, I've found that most conflict boils down to a usual culprit: Who's right and who's wrong?

As you know by now, my college years were full of tasks and deadlines. There were two things I had to come to grips with from my college fraternity experience. One was that people are indeed different from each other. The other is that there's really no such thing as right or wrong. Life is lived in the gray zone, not in black or white. My whole world view was black and white, right and wrong. That is, until I was propelled into a situation where I couldn't control all the variables and had to work with other people.

What we perceive to be right or truth is rooted in our own past experiences and environment, nature vs. nurture. Thus we develop beliefs as to what is right or wrong based on these two factors. Then you bring in your temperament, and you realize that truth in most instances is subjective.

Now, this isn't to say that you should abandon rules, times, and policies. Your organization probably wouldn't last if people missed deadlines. I mean, imagine what would happen if a big grocery chain didn't get their shipment of Coca-Cola right before the July 4th holiday. Think of the catastrophic possibilities if the tower guys at the airport didn't let pilots know the precise moment they were supposed to change coordinates. We must have some degree of order.

But as a leader you have to know when rules can be bent. You have to know when people come before policies.

You've already heard about my "punctuality" escapades with my fraternity. If we were having our monthly frat meeting and the start time was at 3 p.m., my truth was that you needed to be there five to ten minutes prior to the start time because that was only right, to me.

If my line brothers were told they'd be picked up at 2:15, my expectation was that they'd be ready and waiting at 2:10, and that at 2:15 we'd be on our way. For me, this was right, and anything other than my perception was wrong.

Now let's examine my subjective interpretation of truth. Where did I get my definition of truth? My dad.

He didn't believe in living in the gray; he was a black-and-white type of guy. So that meant if he said we were leaving for church at 10 a.m., he would be pulling out of the driveway at 10 a.m. Consequently this meant we needed to be dressed and ready to go prior to 10 a.m. Typically we'd be ready at 9:45, as most times leaving at 10 a.m. would turn out to be 9:56 a.m. In our attempts to avoid a verbal rebuke, we were spit-and-polished ready 15 minutes early most of the time.

Sometimes we got left. But that was Dad's way. If I had to stay after school for basketball practice that was over at 4:30 and my Dad was picking me up, I could bank on him being there at 4:15, nine times out of ten.

My environment taught me that being on time was 10 to 15 minutes early, and that anything else was unacceptable. Thus my interpretation of right and wrong, acceptable or unacceptable was formed at a very early age. So when I began to deal with other people, I assumed they held the same truths that I had. I also assumed that if they violated my interpretation of right, they would be expecting and okay with a verbal attack. That's how things were handled in my house. That's how I handled things in every relationship I had. I felt justified in my actions always. Unfortunately I couldn't have been more mistaken or misguided in my actions.

A mentor once told me not to be so smart that I'm dumb.

In other words, I was so sure that the way I saw things was correct that I failed to acknowledge that other people had their own past experiences as well. It was arrogance, I must admit. Blind arrogance that resulted in lots of hurt feelings, busted relationships, and aborted business deals—mainly because I thought my way was the only way.

My elementary school friend, Thomas, showed me the flaw in that thinking and consequently gave me a great leadership lesson and gift. Thomas was raised by a single mom. His mom worked two jobs, doing the best with what she had. Her life wasn't as regimented and structured as mine. As a result, when Thomas's mom said she'd pick him up at 4:30, it was the norm for her to arrive at 5:00 or later.

It won't surprise you that I had perfect attendance and not one tardy in elementary school. Thomas was always in detention because he was regularly dropped off late at school.

His environment taught him that being on time was relative. I can't say that punctuality wasn't important to him, but I can see how it wasn't as important to him as it was to me, simply because of his experience. He probably was glad when his mom was only 30 minutes late. I would've been a basket case had my dad been even five minutes tardy. It was just a difference in experiences.

So when I attacked him for not being on time, as I often did, I was attacking his truth. I was essentially attacking him. Guess what he did in response? He blocked me. Not only did he block me, he also developed a negative opinion of me, thereby blocking my ability to connect with him and effectively lead him.

Now I know what all of my fellow black-and-white, left-brain fanatics are thinking, "Ten o'clock means 10 o'clock." To you, there is no gray; this is clearly a black-and-white, right-or-wrong situation.

Congratulations, you're right. But right or wrong isn't the point. And being stuck on right and wrong isn't the path to great leadership. Being right isn't why you're the boss. Being right isn't your purpose as Mom or Dad. Being right isn't why you're the pastor. The reason you should be in your leadership role is because of your ability to accomplish the task at hand—your ability to be productive. If accomplishing the task is your ultimate goal, sometimes you may have to put being right to the side.

Nobody likes someone who fights to be right. Nobody follows (for the long haul) a leader whose sole agenda is to be right. Nobody will put their own ego aside for someone who, at the end of the day, cares about one thing: being right.

You need people. You can't lead without them. If imposing your definition of right on someone else impedes your ability to accomplish the task, you must let it go. That doesn't mean you don't address the issue, but it does mean you're wise enough to know when, where, and how to do it.

A TIME TO KILL

Rodney comes to the meeting late, and we've been waiting on the estimate for the cost of the venue to determine where we'd host the after-party for our annual non-Greek step show.

The goal? To determine which venue will host the step show after-party.

Rodney walks in at 3:25 for a three o'clock meeting. Here is how the conversation would go.

Me: "Say, man, where've you been? It's almost 3:30!"

Rodney: "It's only 3:20! Relax D-Dot."

Me: "The meeting started at three o'clock. Do you have those numbers on the venues?"

Rodney: "I'll have them tomorrow."

Me: "You said you'd have them today. We can't lock in a venue without those numbers."

Rodney: "You'll have them tomorrow."

Now, let's look at what is really being said in this exchange with Rodney.

Rodney walks in at 3:25 for the three o'clock meeting.

What's Said: "Say man, where have you been? It's almost 3:30!"

What Is Really Meant: "Being on time is the right thing that good and decent people like me value."

What's Said: "It's only 3:20!"

What Is Really Meant: "What's wrong with being 20 minutes late? You always try to act like you are always right and I'm tired of it."

What's Said: "The meeting started at three o'clock. Do you have those numbers on the venues?"

What Is Really Meant: "You should have been on time, but obviously you are too stupid to realize it. So let's move on to see if you can do anything right. Do you have the numbers?"

What's Said: "I'll have them tomorrow."

What Is Really Meant: "Yeah, I got the numbers, but I'm going to make you wait out of spite. I'm launching a covert attack."

What's Said: "You said you'd have them today. We can't lock in a venue without those numbers."

What Is Really Meant: "Obviously your word means nothing to you and your thinking is warped. As a result of your actions, we can't lock in the venue like we were supposed to."

What's Said: "Okay, you'll have them tomorrow."

What Is Really Meant: "Mission accomplished. I pissed you off. Heck, I may even wait until the day after tomorrow because you get on my nerves!"

Productive or unproductive? Yep, highly unproductive. Heck, this is beyond unproductive; it's downright dysfunctional. Unfortunately, more times than not, this is how we tend to operate in our relationships.

PRODUCTIVITY MODEL

Using the same scenario, let's see how this would play out using the productivity model.

Rodney walks in at 3:25 for the three o'clock meeting.

Me: "Hey Rodney, what's up, frat? We were just about to discuss the venue for the show. Did you get those numbers?"

Rodney: "Yeah, here you go!"

This scenario is a lot shorter and much more efficient. As a leader I was focused on what was important in the moment: the quote for the venue. As the leader, you set the tone. If you start off in condemnation, you can expect condemnation to follow. On the other hand, if you lead in productivity, you'll likely have a more productive outcome.

Now let's see what could be going through the mind of each individual in this conversation.

Rodney walks in at 3:25 for the three o'clock meeting.

What's Said: "Hey Rodney, what's up, frat? We were just about to discuss the venue for the show. Did you get those numbers?"

What I'm Thinking: "Rodney is late again, but if I call him out right here in front of everyone, it'll just lead to an argument. This will result in us not accomplishing the task at hand, so for the sake of the task, I'll let it go and focus on the task."

What's Said: "Yeah, here you go!"

What He's Thinking: "Man, I know I should have been here earlier. I'm surprised Jerome didn't call me out. Let me do my part and provide the numbers."

Now, I don't want you to get the idea that leaders should avoid conflict. Not at all. Remember, conflict is essential to growth. But leaders must discern when to dive into discussions about behaviors. It's all about the timing of the discussion. If someone's done something that violates the rules of your culture, they must be held accountable. Failure to address the behavior will likely lead to more of the same behavior. So the goal is not to avoid talking about it; the goal is to be selective about when to talk about it.

KIDS DO THE DARNDEST THINGS

It's human nature to want to be liked. From the day we were born, we were seeking approval and affirmation. Having four children will challenge the leader in you, trust me. Sometimes I revert to habits of negative reinforcement. This model isn't concerned as much with productivity, but tends to result in condemnation.

When my son was only three, his three older sisters were five, six, and eight, and they all had chores. Their chores varied from wiping the dinner table to sweeping the floors to dusting. They all got feedback—hugs and high fives from me after completing their chores. My son saw the level of attention they received, and he wanted to get some of Dad's attention too. So I gave him a simple chore.

Our kids typically leave their cups on the table all day. When they're running around the house playing and they get thirsty, they can simply go over and get some water. My son's new chore was to make sure all the cups were put in the sink at the end of the day before they all went to bed.

For the first couple of weeks he was Johnny on the Spot. Right after everyone ate dinner, he'd run to the kitchen and toss the cups in the sink. Then he'd come to me and announce, "Daddy, I did my chore." Now there was no requirement to tell me when he did his chore, but he took it upon himself to make the announcement. Why? Because he wanted to be recognized. He wanted to be appreciated. He wanted the same accolades his sisters got when they did their chores.

A few weeks passed, and I suspect the chore thing had lost its shine in my son's eyes. So he started to slack off. He apparently started to value his playtime more than his chore time. After all, he was three years old. I noticed his lack of enthusiasm for the cups and instead of reprimanding him and telling him how disappointed I was that he hadn't been diligent in his chores, I took a different approach.

I began to encourage and speak "desired actions" into his life. So when he would miss his assignment, and even at times when he didn't, I'd say things like, "Man! L.J. is always focused. I can depend upon him to do his chore. I'm proud of you, son. You always do your chore without me having to tell you. Great job." I encouraged what I wanted to see in him. Guess what L.J. Did? He became more consistent in doing his chore.

After a few instances of getting encouragement, he started to really step up with his game, not just because he wanted my attention but because he saw himself as one that didn't need to be told what to do. He started to exhibit his own brand of leadership.

Interestingly enough, his reputation became important to him, and he didn't want to let me down. You may think, sure, Love, that works for children, but guess what? It works with adults as well.

Let's say you've got a team member who recently has been short with customers. Your company has a great reputation of taking care of customers in fine fashion. But this one staff member seems to have gotten some negative feedback on their customer calls.

Instead of pointing out how detrimental their behavior is to the company's well-being, you might say something like this: "One of the reasons we wanted you on the floor is that we know how great you are with the customers. I noticed a couple pieces of interesting feedback and wanted to see if there's anything going on I should know about that would result in feedback that's unlike your customary feedback."

Then, just shut up. Let the staff member talk. You haven't condemned him or her. You haven't accused them of being wrong. You haven't threatened to demerit them. You haven't forced your "black-and-white" view on them. You've simply asked a question. So, just listen.

By acknowledging their good work prior to asking them to give you insights on their recent feedback, you've kept the window of communication open. You've shown them you're an advocate for their success. You've avoided the deadly shame, blame, guilt, and defensive dance most bosses do with their employees. More importantly, you've kept the conversation positive, and you've shown respect for whatever might be going on with them. You've done what I call distracted them with a compliment. Additionally, you're building an image they'll want to maintain.

Successful leaders understand the psychology of human change and transformation. They know that conflict is not to be averted but rather embraced. The great ones know that when they seek first to understand, they not only invite understanding in return, but they also create a culture where conflict is used to grow rather than destroy the team and its

117

vision. Before I sign off on this powerful concept of conflict resolution, I'd be remiss if I didn't talk about two more of my favorite leadership laws: The Law of Apology and The Law of Cancellation.

LOVE'S LAW OF LEADERSHIP

Law of Apology

If you screw something up, you take public responsibility for it through a sincere apology.

Sometimes in conflict, there's a need for retribution. I don't know why the word "apology" leaves such a bad taste on folks' palates, but it often does. If you're one of those leaders who walks around wreaking havoc and leaving your team to clean up after your tornado, listen up.

The Law of Apology simply states that if you screw something up, you take public responsibility for it through a sincere apology. A genuine apology might go something like this: Let's say you accuse a coworker of not pulling their weight on a project. You're under the gun and feeling so much pressure you don't even take the time to hear their side of the story. When the dust settles, you learn that what you thought had happened, had not exactly happened. Now you've got to eat a Texas-size plate of crow. You might be tempted to send out a memo acknowledging your mistake. Not a smart first move. A great leader's *first* move is to apologize directly to the individual or individuals you've offended with your unproductive leadership behavior.

Your apology doesn't have to be long and drawn out, but it most definitely should be sincere. "Kathy, I made a mistake. I accused you of something you didn't do and I apologize.

My behavior is inconsistent with our values, and I hope you can forgive me."

That's it. That's a solid, genuine apology that addresses your actions and expresses remorse and contrition.

LOVE'S LAW OF LEADERSHIP

Law of Cancellation

If you apologize and then immediately explain why you did what you did, it cancels the apology.

Now, what you'll find in your personal and professional relationships is that most people will not stop there. They'll move right into violating my next law, The Law of Cancellation, which states that if you apologize and then immediately explain *why* you did what you did, it cancels the apology.

Don't do it. It negates the apology.

Take for instance the situation of a late employee. He comes in late to a major meeting. He later apologizes for being late, offering what will surely be perceived as a lame excuse, "I didn't know traffic was going to be that bad. Usually on Jefferson if flows pretty smooth."

You see, the mind is a tricky thing. And what most people don't understand is that your mind works for you. If you're a prideful person, your mind works overtime to ensure that you're right at all costs. So in the "cancellation" statement, what's ultimately being communicated is, "It wasn't my fault. I was late because of traffic."

If I heard that apology, I'd have very little confidence that this behavior wouldn't happen in the future as the employee made it clear that his tardiness was not a result of anything he did or didn't do. As stated, it was all out of his control.

Contrast the apology above with this one: "I'm sorry I was late. I'll just have to leave 15 minutes earlier from now on to ensure I am here on time. Sorry I held up the meeting." That's ownership. That's accountability. And that apology also includes a solution for not making the same mistake twice.

My point is that in life and in leadership you *will* make mistakes. Hopefully, you'll be big enough to recognize your mistakes and own up to them. Because as tough as it may be to eat humble pie, people will accept you making mistakes if you own them by admitting your humanity and making every effort to be better going forward.

PART II TAKEAWAYS

- Conflict is a necessary part of growth and shouldn't be avoided.

- Conflict resolution is a critical skill for leaders.

- Create an environment where conflict is not a win-loss proposition.

- Model productive communication skills and habits, and your team will follow you.

- There is no right and wrong in conflict—only what's best for the relationship.

- Don't be so married to "your way" that you lose sight of what's going to get you the results you desire.

- Diversity of thought is the fuel needed to grow your company and relationships.

- Don't seek to attract people like you; seek to align yourself with people who bring different perspectives because that's when the magic starts.

- Resolving conflict often means apologizing and re-calibrating the relationship so that you can reset on a positive and productive note.

- Law of Attack: If a person is attacked, they will defend themselves.

- Law of Apology: If you screw something up, you take public responsibility for it through a sincere apology

- Law of Cancellation: If you apologize and then immediately explain why you did what you did, it cancels the apology.

PART III: INFLUENCE

Influence
The ability to be a
compelling force in the
decisions, actions,
behaviors, and beliefs
of others.

WANGIN' IT

Electronics have to be one of the most competitive industries to enter, so what in the world would compel someone to make TVs in 2013? That's the question I asked myself as I was reading about Vizio founder, William Wang. It just doesn't make any sense. But then Wang doesn't care a whole lot about the sensical.

Wang was one of the 96 survivors aboard a Singapore Airlines 747 that took off on the wrong runway in Taiwan in 2000. Death stared him straight in the eyes and he lived to talk about it. So making sense is the last thing on Wang's agenda's these days. He's all about innovating, influencing, and making a difference.

Based in Irvine, California, Wang believed he could influence consumers into thinking about their television purchases in a different way. He was right. Starting his company with $600,000 and the crazy notion to sell big TVs for lower than most market prices, his gamble's paid off. His company will generate close to $2 billion in sales this year. Yes, that's billions with a "b," employing only 80 people. Innovative? Sure. Influential? Absolutely.

Now, you might be saying, "Cool story, J. Love, but I don't see what selling TVs has to do with influence." So let's go a little deeper.

Wang entered a highly saturated marketplace: consumer electronics. A category with well-established players like Sony, Life is Good, Toshiba, and others. In order to build a successful company, Wang's Vizio would have to do more than build a better television and offer it at a cheaper price;

they'd also have to convince millions of consumers to take a chance and switch from iconic brands Sony and Toshiba to Vizio. Are you crazy?

In order to achieve what I just described, Wang and his team had to become masters at everything I've talk about so far in *Love Them and Lead Them*. They had to understand the needs of television-buying consumers. They had to find out what consumers needed and wanted from a big-screen television. They had to find out what was currently missing in the marketplace that would influence a potential prospect to consider Vizio (another form of conflict resolution). And last but certainly not least, Wang's bunch had to persuade consumers to pull out their credit cards and actually buy an unproven brand when other mega brands of TVs were available to them. If that's not influence, I don't know what to tell ya!

Influence Demystified

The Vizio story just scratched the surface of what we're about discuss in this section. There are three things that must happen before you can positively and effectively influence others.

- You must have or develop a relationship with them that's based on some level of trust.

- You must understand what motivates them to take action.

- You must communicate with them in a way that underscores #1 and #2.

The rate at which you'll be able to influence them will depend on your proficiency at these three things.

> Sure, I could complicate the requirements—even add more steps—but truthfully, they'd still all boil down to your ability to develop relationships, understand why people do what they do, and talk to them so they'll listen ... and take action

WHAT DALE KNEW

Renowned speaker and thought leader Dale Carnegie nailed it in his best-selling book *How to Win Friends and Influence People.*

I always wondered why he chose the phrase "win friends." That phrase always struck me as odd. But the more I evolved as a leader, the more I understood the psychology behind the word "friend." Some words in our vocabulary carry such heavy connotations. "Friend" is one of those.

Consider the emotional currency of this sentence: Tim is one of my best friends in the whole world. Or, what about this one: Yes, I'm acquainted with Tim, but we're not friends. You see what I mean? There's a visceral difference between those two statements. Without knowing me or Tim, you already know a lot about our relationship just through the use of the word "friend."

Carnegie knew that we humans identify strongly with the word "friend." He could have titled his book *How to Influence People and Become Successful.* It doesn't have quite the same resonance as winning friends. He also cleverly used the word "win" to get people's attention. He catered to the thrill-seeker in all of us. We love victory. Most of us thrive on competition. And all of us love winning.

How to Win Friends and Influence People has sold more than 15 million copies worldwide and became the forefather of books on influence and leadership. Thank you, Mr. Carnegie, for leading the way.

THE POWER IN PROMISES

What we're really talking about here is persuasion. I recently asked a group of students to define "persuasion," and more than half of them said, "Getting people to do what you want them to do." Some said, "Getting people to do what you want them to do and making them think it was their idea." All interesting concepts, but the problem with those kinds of definitions is that it feels like manipulation, which isn't what true leadership's about.

I understand what the students were getting at; I simply want to draw a definitive line in the sand when it comes to distinguishing between manipulating followers and leading them.

An extreme example of what can happen when manipulation and fear are thrown into the conversation and blended with leadership is Adolf Hitler. Some will say Hitler was a great leader because he was not only able to get people to follow him, but because he also almost single handedly changed the course of history.

I don't hail what Hitler did as leadership although clearly his actions were persuasive. I use him in the section on influence because there are portions of his German reign that are useful in the discussion on influence.

Germany was in trouble. They had been hit hard by the Great Depression. Hitler knew this. He knew that Germans were in pain. He knew they wanted redemption and recovery. So essentially he used public pain to get the public's attention. Nothing new here yet. That's the basis of all great marketing—figure out the pain points and promise solutions.

Notice I didn't say "provide" solutions; I said promise solutions. Isn't that what great campaigns are about? That's how every president of the United States campaigns. That's what every high school class president campaigns behind. Promises.

Hitler's promises were clear: I will make Germany great again. I will end Communism. I will create economic recovery—jobs. On these three promises, Hitler built a wicked but very influential reign. Let's examine the power in his promises because they reveal how you, as a leader, are potentially able to influence those in your charge.

Promise #1: I will make Germany great again.

This apparently was music to the ears of a war-ravaged nation. A nation in pain. A nation full of despair. A nation thirsty for hope. Enter Hitler with his "We'll be great again" campaign promise.

Promise #2: I will end Communism.

Many Germans believed Communism was the root of their pain. As much as it was revered by many during the time, it was also considered the bane of many existences. Enter Hitler with his "I will end Communism (your pain)" promises.

Promise #3: I will create jobs.

It's been said that what keeps a nation (even today) embroiled in despair is the inability to take care of itself economically. A country that feels economically destitute is bound to riot, is bound to revolt. Hitler knew this. He knew that Germany had been hit hard by the Great Depression. He knew his campaign rallies would be filled with individuals who were tired of the status quo and eager for change.

Let me make it clear that I do not endorse Hitler or his tactics, but I ask you, "What can you as a leader learn from Hitler?" You don't need to condone his manipulative and horrific antics to be able to extract something positive. I'll share three key nuggets:

First, effective leadership ultimately comes down to possessing unstoppable confidence. I'm not saying that Hitler always believed he'd successfully torture six million Jews. But I'm certain that at some point he began to notice he was having great success persuading people to agree with his beliefs and actions toward Jews.

It started with his oratory skills. Most accounts of Hitler talk about his ability to arouse audiences. He was charismatic. He was convicted. It wasn't so much about what he said; it was more about how he said it. The same holds true today.

LOVE'S LAW OF LEADERSHIP

Law of Help

People feel significant when they're able to help someone else.

If we were to research recent presidential campaigns, you'd find that most of them are won by the man who is the best orator. There are instances when the best orator did not win, but you can count those on one hand. It's certainly true for our last two presidential campaigns. Aside from his social media and marketing prowess, President Barack Obama electrified a nation through eloquence and delivery. The man who can command the room typically wins. He's the guy or gal who can connect with the masses, the person who understands and speaks to the pain of the people.

Obama also exercised my Law of Help: People feel significant when they're able to help someone else. Political campaigns use this one to the hilt. "I need your help to change America," or "With your help we can make America great again." Subtle but powerful ways to help people feel significant. When people feel like they've helped, they feel empowered. Their egos are stroked and they feel significant. But that's not all. If you gave them the opportunity to experience that significance, you've now also boosted your influence.

I recently had to write a letter to about 30 elected officials the other day to request their help in promoting The Texas Black Expo. My opening line was: **I need your help.** Now, unless you're completely self-centered, you're not going to ignore those four words staring at you. You're going to read on to see how you can help.

How can you use this strategy for greater influence at home or work? Find something that a person's good at, commend them for it, and then ask them, "Can you show me how to do that one day?" or "Would you be willing to teach the team how to do that at our next meeting?" Watch how their eyes light up as they pull out their smartphone to check their calendar availability.

You've not only just made a huge goodwill deposit that not only made them feel more valuable and important, but you've also cashed a big fat check into the Bank of Influence. Nice job.

Love's 5 Tenets of Influence

Whether we're talking about consumer behavior or religious obedience, influence is at work all day every day.

Did you know that a mint could influence the amount of a restaurant tip? It's true. Research has shown that when a mint is left with the diner's check, tips are increased by 3 to 4 percent. If the waiter leaves one mint and turns back and says something such as, "Ooops, because you were such a great customer, I'm going to give you an extra one," the tip is increased by 15 percent.

But why?

Because of our first leadership tenet: Reciprocity.

The notion that I'll give to you if you give to me is a powerful tool. It's at work even when we don't know it's at work.

We are wired to respond to people who "give to us." Ever wondered why predators often begin grooming their prey with gifts? Because it ignites a feeling of returned generosity. Creepy but true. People who give to us are hypnotizing us to give back to them.

Now, how does this work in leadership? Well, as leaders we're put in the position to give and reward almost immediately. We reward with words, promotions, and awards. These actions create a sense of indebtedness in the person receiving our generosity. Consider these actions that appear to be simple acts of kindness.

1. A CEO brings donuts to the office each morning. What do her followers think? Awww, that's sweet. I'm going to work harder for her this quarter. She's always so thoughtful. She didn't have to do this. She must really care about me.

2. A sports coach gives a team the day off. What does his team think of this act? Whoa, Coach is cool. I sure need a day off. He must've have known. He's in tune with what we need. He <u>does</u> care about us. I'm going to go hard next practice.

3. A pastor builds a daycare for her parishioners. What's the flock thinking? God has sent us an angel who puts our needs first. I'm going to sow an extra 2 percent next month.

Now, these may seem like minor considerations, but I challenge you to reread them to see how, if nurtured properly, they become seeds of massive influence.

Next, there's scarcity.

This is the notion that if there's only a little of it, we'll want it more.

How many times have you been inspired to drive to Walmart in the middle of the night on Christmas Eve because they announced they had a shipment of only 120 50-inch plasma TVs? Or better yet, how many of you have stood in line outside the Apple Store waiting to get the next iPhone or iPad?

Your fear of not getting what you want motivated you, influenced you to engage in some pretty interesting, borderline nutty behavior, right? Scarcity is a powerful tool in leadership. Leveraging it to drive sales or even desirable behavior is a long-held practice in companies around the globe. As a leader you can drive productive behavior through scarcity by giving people the opportunity to attend a highly desirable event if they achieve certain departmental goals.

It's not uncommon for airlines to threaten to stop service to a particular destination to simply drive consumption.

That's right. There were likely never any plans to stop going from Roanoke to Nashville; the airlines just told you that to get you to make reservations. Powerful.

Other companies will host a contest to give away one vacation a year to drive employees to crank up their efforts. Employees will kick it into high gear not only because they want to be recognized but also because they fear they'll miss out on the opportunity of a lifetime.

How else might you be able to use scarcity in an ethical way to gain additional influence?

THE THIRD TENET OF INFLUENCE IS LIKEABILITY.

We've all heard that people do business with people they know, like, and trust. Likeability just might be the Ace of Spades in the trio. That's why if influence is your goal, you can never underestimate the power of being liked. Don't let anybody tell you any differently; it IS a popularity contest in most companies. The top leaders who are liked more by their teams typically make more money and are perceived more favorably than those who are not.

So how do you become more likeable? Well, that's where I believe the other two spades come in: know and trust.

Clearly, it's not possible for the average person to truly KNOW the President of the United States, yet some candidates somehow feel very familiar to us. The more familiar they are to us, the more chances we have to like them. That's why if you've done any marketing online, you'll always see a sales page start out with the product creator sharing what I call their "tragedy to triumph" story. People want to know about the mess before we hear the message. It's what breaks down the barriers between people.

When we know about your pain, we feel like we know you—even when we don't. So likeability is a critical element in influence. I learned this the hard way.

When I joined my fraternity, I was second vice president. Mr. Punctuality. Mr. Organization. Some probably called me Mr. Anal behind my back. Even though these qualities worked for me in many cases, in other instances they did not. When it came to leadership, you might think these qualities got me high marks. Surprisingly, they did not. Not because they aren't good qualities but because alone, they're pretty self-serving. The way I embodied these qualities actually did more to divide than bring people together. Sometimes your view of yourself can become so distorted that you become even more self-righteousness and judgmental, wondering why everyone else is not like you. Ever felt that way?

I wasn't very social. In fact, I was downright unsocial. As a result, many of the older brothers or prophytes didn't like me. I was labeled as un-fraternal. Why? Because I didn't hang out. I didn't party with them. I would skip the hellos when I walked into an event or meeting and cut straight to business. This is the way my nurture wired me.

I didn't realize it at the time, but my inability and un-willingness to "fraternize" with my older frat was severely hampering my productivity and ability to influence and lead them. I didn't have an influential relationship with them, and I didn't understand why. I thought I represented everything that was Alpha.

As I look back now, the prophytes didn't know me. The neophytes were the guys that pledged with me. We lived together in the same house for more than six weeks, so these guys knew me. They knew I was reliable, they knew I was witty, and at the end of the day, they knew I had the fraternity's best interests at heart, thus I connected with them because of our relationship. But there was still a disconnect with me and the prophytes.

The prophytes didn't get to see who the neophytes got to see. They only saw me barking orders and yelling at folks who were late to meetings. They never got to see any other side of me, and for a while this had a profoundly negative impact on my ability to influence and connect with them. You guessed it; my stubbornness was about to lead to more roller-coaster rides and a bevy of leadership lessons.

Tim, one of my best friends who was also a line brother, was the exact opposite of me. Uber sociable. People loved him. Because we were so close and lived together, when people saw me, they always saw Tim. We'd go to a meeting and before I could greet everyone, they'd interrupt me and say, "Where's Tim?"

Did I notice the difference in how folks responded to Tim? Of course. It was impossible not to. Tim was like a rock star. But honestly I was so relationally dysfunctional that I really didn't care, or so I told myself. I was about getting it done, whatever "it" was. I didn't have time for all that touchy-feely stuff that I thought was for losers.

Instead of looking in the mirror, I told myself that the people who couldn't get on the Jerome Love approach to life simply couldn't appreciate good leadership. It wasn't until years later, after I founded the Texas Black Expo, that I started to get a clue about how to build solid relationships. In studying Tim's influence I began to notice subtle but distinct differences in how people perceived us. He was open. He was emotionally available, so it was easy for people to connect with him. What I now know is that Tim was modeling how to become a better leader.

THE FOURTH TENET IS AUTHORITY, AND IT'S A BIGGIE.

Authority simply means the leader's seen as more credible than the next person on the totem pole. It doesn't mean the leader's actually the smartest person in the room or on the team. It means that followers have confidence in the leader's ability to take them where they want to go. The Bible talks about what a great leader Moses became, but it also reveals that Moses questioned why God thought he was a good candidate to lead the Israelites out of Egypt. Moses didn't see his leadership abilities or potential the way God did.

He pointed out all the reasons he shouldn't be the leader. He even gave God a list of men who he thought were better for the job. But once Moses embraced his inner leader, he was able to gain the confidence of his people and lead them out of bondage. It was his position and perception of authority that made them walk through the Red Sea with Moses.

The more authority you are believed to have, the more influence you'll have. Your authority is cemented more in your followers' minds if the expression of your feats comes from third parties. Let me repeat that.

Your authority is cemented more in your followers' minds if the expression of your feats comes from third parties.

You can't walk around the office telling everyone how great you are. That wouldn't be very effective. But if those same followers walked around the company and heard or saw evidence of your feats, your authority wouldn't be questioned. Ever notice how an office buzzes when a bigwig's coming to town? Their reputation precedes them. Their authority solidifies their influence.

Drop Down and Give Me 20

You wanna talk about influence? Nobody saw fitness phenom, P90X, coming.

It's now a near-billion-dollar fitness program that promises you ripped abs and chiseled bodies without ever having to leave the comfort of your home. The program's sold almost exclusively online and via late-night television infomercials starring creator Tony Horton.

Now, when the show first comes on (at 2 a.m.), Tony doesn't come on screen telling you why his program's the best. Instead, a third-party voiceover guy does. He explains why Tony's methodologies put all the other guys' stuff to shame. Once the voiceover guy's sufficiently conveyed Tony's authority, then, and only then, does Tony appear on screen (ripped and shredded) to speak to the TV audience.

But wait, there's more!

Tony tells us why you need to pull out your credit card, but then he allows about 10 other regular Joes and Janes to tell you, in their own words, how Tony's program has transformed their bodies and their lives. There's the stay-at-home mom who wanted to lose her baby weight. There's the ex-athlete guy who gained 50 pounds. There's the girl who's never run a marathon but got the courage and strength to do it after following the P90X plan and workout. These testimonials are more than case studies; they're confirmations of Tony's and P90X's authority.

THE FIFTH AND FINAL TENET IS SOCIAL PRESSURE.

Most people would like to think they can operate outside the box, but most of us prefer to move in pairs and groups. We like the safety that comes with being in a tribe. That's why social pressure's such a powerful, influential mechanism. In fact, it's arguably the one tenet that truly allowed Hitler to take over Germany.

There was likely a time during Hitler's tyranny that people thought, "Wait a minute. This can't be right. This is not going to end well. I should say something." Yet the pressure to go along with the group-think mentality was enormous, and clearly so dangerous, that no one dared stand up to the Nazi regime.

Hitler undoubtedly knew there would come a time of critical mass. A time when his army of hate would be so strong that even the few who thought about standing up to him would back down.

LOVE'S 10 HABITS OF HIGHLY INFLUENTIAL LEADERS

Go to the bookstore today and you'll see more than a dozen leadership books and even more magazine articles on the topic. It's true; great leaders possess a multitude of compelling qualities when it comes to influence. I call these my 10 Habits of Highly Influential Leaders.

HABIT #1: INTEGRITY

Ask 53 people what integrity is and you might get at least 43 different answers. Integrity can't be defined simply but most people typically agree on actions that are not aligned with integrity: People who say one thing and do another. People who behave one way in the company of certain people and then change who they are when others are around. So, you might call integrity the consistency of actions and words by an individual or organization.

Do you operate with integrity? Are you an honest person? If not, plan on having a hard time being a successful leader. When I conduct leadership trainings, I often do an interactive illustration on leadership. It starts with inviting three people to the front.

I put the tallest or biggest one in the middle, the shortest one in back, and the other person in front. The person in the middle represents you, the leader. The person behind represents the status quo, or in this case, the follower. The person in front is the dream, vision, or goal. Then I ask, "Why would you ask this person," pointing to the person behind him, "about your dream or vision?"

Then I ask the last person in line if they can see the dream or vision, to which they respond "No." I then ask, "Why can't you see the vision?" The answer is, they can't see around the leader. (Remember, this is the tallest and biggest one.) The leader is the one out front. The leader is the one that has a clear sight on the vision.

Here's the beef. If the follower is to continue to follow you to a place they can't clearly see for themselves, there must be a certain level of trust. This trust is based first and foremost upon your integrity.

Now to understand this concept fully I want to piggyback on an illustration I've seen author Chris Widener do on several occasions. Widener is also a member of the Republican party and was a candidate for the US Senate in 2010 in Washington State.

Think back to high school math. What term did you learn that almost sounds like integrity? The answer's integer. Now the real question is do you remember what an integer is? Nope?

An integer is a whole number. It's a Latin term that means untouched, whole or complete. People that operate with integrity are whole people. Typically people lie to cover a certain perceived deficiency in their life. There's a level of vulnerability they don't want exposed. They are not whole; they lack self-esteem or pride in themselves, thus they lie to try to make themselves look better.

Now let's look at it from another perspective. The opposite of being whole is to be divided. Would you want to follow a divided leader? One day he says one thing and the next it's something different? Do you smile in a person's face and commend them, and then when they leave, do you talk bad about them? Are your actions complete or are they divided?

As I mentioned earlier, children will challenge your leadership skills. They learn at a very early age about integrity and divided behavior. They know when you're not being completely honest. Like many kids, mine love sugar. Cake, cookies, cupcakes—they're addicted to all of it. I wanted to teach them that eating sweets was not good for them; however, I didn't want to focus only on the negative.

I'd read a book about turning negatives into positives, so instead of telling them they couldn't eat sweets, I decided to tell them when they *could* eat sweets. So every first and third Saturday is Sweets Saturday at the Love house. This small switch changed everything. Now the kids have something to look forward to, as opposed to the negative perception of something they could not have.

This system worked pretty well for maybe a month, then I have to be honest, my behavior became a bit divided. From time to time, when the kids would go to bed, I'd have the occasional bowl of ice cream, a brownie, or a cookie. I rationalized my behavior like most divided leaders. I'd tell myself my behavior was completely in integrity. After all, I was the "Dad" (like that made it okay).

As I was sneaking in the freezer for my treats, I'd say, "They're asleep. They'll never know." Boy, was I wrong. After a few weeks of my divided behavior, they began to notice the ice cream was diminishing or that there were fewer cookies in the cookie jar in the morning when they got out of bed.

One day while I was watching TV, all four of them marched downstairs in one unified front.

"Daddy, we want some ice cream. You said we could only have sweet on the first and third Saturday, but when we go to bed, you're eating sweets!"

I was busted, and you haven't been busted until you've been busted by a four-year old.

I wanted to tell them "I was the Daddy!" but I knew they were right. My ability to lead my family into healthier eating habits was being jeopardized because of my lack of integrity.

That's one of my leadership secrets. What's one of yours? Mine was after-hours ice cream; what about you? What are you doing to undermine your leadership? What are you doing that you think your followers don't know about? Trust me, they know. And if they don't yet know, they'll find out sooner than you think.

INTEGRITY TIPS

#1 Do what you say. Don't be divided in your words and actions.

#2 Tell the truth. People will not follow someone they do not trust. Period.

#3 Make an apology. If you know you have operated in a manner that lacks integrity, make an apology.

It's okay to make a mistake, but it's not okay to do nothing about it. One of the hardest things to do is to admit when you're wrong. When you do wrong, the other person knows it, whether you admit it or not. Admitting your flaws and making a sincere apology will boost your integrity tremendously in the eyes of those you offend.

Too many people are concerned with looking weak by apologizing. Great leaders understand that apologies are a necessary part of maintaining respect with those who follow you. There's no quicker way to lose their respect than by offending them and not acknowledging your offense.

HABIT #2: APPRECIATE

> *"There are two things people want more than sex and money ... recognition and praise."*
> **Mary Kay Ash**

Jack Canfield said it best in his book *The Success Principles:* A state of appreciation is one of the highest vibrational emotional states. But there's a trio of other actions leaders should take to increase their influence: recognize, acknowledge, and compliment. Those aren't nouns; they're verbs.

When appreciation's a priority, organizations, teams, and families soar. Imagine if your friends never said thanks.

Or if your spouse never rubbed your feet after a long day. Or if your kids never hugged you. You'd feel pretty under-appreciated, wouldn't you? Most of us would.

So, it boggles my mind that more leaders don't show more appreciation for the folks they're privileged to lead.

In 2005, I sold a house for a gentleman by the name of Lee Davis. In fact, I may have done too good of a job as his house sold in two days. Because of this, Lee had to scramble to find another place to live.

As a result of the sale, he started sending me referral after referral. After about the third or fourth referral, I became overwhelmed by his generosity, and I wanted to really show my appreciation.

I didn't know Lee very well, other than as a client, and I wanted my token of appreciation to be special, so I started asking folks who knew him well. I called this guy named Lofton and said, "Man, Lee has referred me a ton of new clients. I really want to get him something nice, something he likes, but I really don't know him personally. Got any suggestions?"

Lofton provided a list of a few of Lee's favorite restaurants and then said, "You know, I got a couple deals I can send your way as well." I had subconsciously implanted a desire to send me referrals.

You can use the same concept I use for referrals to increase productivity on your team. If you have an employee or team member that is doing well, talk to another employee that isn't doing so well who knows the one that is. Tell them, "I am really impressed that X person is always on time and always closes their deals. What do you think they would really like?" Without saying a word, in their mind they are thinking about how they could get this special level of appreciation, and they will inherently increase productivity.

HABIT # 3: RECOGNIZE

People will deny they want recognition right up to the moment you recognize everyone except them. I don't care how evolved and how humble an individual, recognition feels good. It's an overt show of appreciation.

Remember the story I shared earlier about my kids and their chores? My son longed for a little recognition. He liked the feeling of being recognized—nothing wrong with that. It motivated him to step up his game.

As leaders you have to know that high salaries, company cars, 401(k)s, and vacations pale in comparison to recognition. Don't every forget that. The recognition doesn't need to be trumpets and rose petals. Hugs and high fives work just fine in some instances.

If you're one of those folks who somehow came up with the silly notion that not recognizing people is the right way to motivate them, think again. Withholding recognition is akin to planting seeds of injustice by depriving them of the natural reward that comes with success.

Another bad habit some leaders possess is claiming credit when they don't deserve it. Nothing will rip through the soul of a good organization or relationship like someone who wants and takes all the glory for the team's success. Share the wealth instead of hogging it. Bring the team to the front of the room and let them share in the applause.

The Big O Recognizes

I'll admit it. I've watched The Oprah Winfrey Show before. Okay, maybe a few times.

Once she launched her cable network, OWN, I saw one of the reality shows called Behind the Scenes. It's a documentary-style show about what it takes to do The Oprah Winfrey Show. I have to admit it was interesting. Fascinating, even.

The world of television is high risk and high reward, but what I found more titillating were all the moving parts it takes to get a show on the air. Booking the guests. Dealing with temper tantrums. Celebrity idiosyncrasies. Hair, makeup, lights, and deadlines.

What the viewing audience sees is Oprah doing her thing in front of the camera, but after watching this 60-minute show, I had a real appreciation for the teamwork it takes to execute an hour-long syndicated talk show.

I respect Oprah for her leadership and success, yes, but this particular show helped me to see just how committed she was to recognizing the individual members of her team, day in and day out. She did little things for them. Took them on vacations. Bought them cars. Treated them with dignity and respect but again, most of all, recognized their contributions to the Oprah Winfrey empire.

No wonder she became a billionaire of influence. She clearly understood and understands who oils her media engine. Her team. Now, maybe you're not in a position to take hundreds of folks on a vacation to Maui, but there's something you can do to show them you care and appreciate them. You just have to figure out what creates the magic in your family or team.

Habit #4: Acknowledge

This is the first cousin to recognize. It's the effort to make mention of someone's contributions. Maybe they didn't carry the weight of the entire project, but they opened the door. So it's a good idea to acknowledge them. Don't wait until a major event to acknowledge their efforts. Weekly meetings are a great place to start.

Sometimes churches are great at acknowledging members (sometimes to a fault). When I was growing up, we'd have regular programs at Easter, Christmas, and other holidays where the kids got to be "on program." It wouldn't matter if there were 10 kids or 35 kids, we all had a part on the Easter program, and we all had our names read to the audience.

Now, you can imagine this took quite a while, but to see the looks on the kids' faces and the expressions on their parents' faces, you knew the acknowledgment had been well worth the wait. It's the same in your situation. Sometimes it's not in good taste to make folks wait hours so that you can read everyone's name as we did in my church. So find an alternative way to recognize your team because it goes a long way in the long run.

Habit #5: Compliment

Most of us are great at handing out insults but terrible at giving genuine compliments. We're stingy with positivity but liberal with negativity. Stop. Right now. Think of five compliments you could pay everyone in your immediate family or office. Can you do it? How long did it take you?

If it took you longer than a few seconds per compliment, you've got some work to do, leader.

Do It Publicly

People are ego driven, so stroke their ego. If you privately call a team member or employee into your office and tell them thank you, or slip a thank you note into their box, that's fine. Imagine how much better they would feel and more productive they would be if, at the weekly sales meeting in front of the whole team, you recognized them and led everyone in a round of applause for that particular person.

Oh, sure, they may be a little uncomfortable at first, but deep down they're loving it. Another added benefit to this overt expression of appreciation and recognition is that you are subconsciously telling the other team members to get it together. You are saying, if you like what Tim's getting, step it up. You could get this level of appreciation too.

Say, "Cheese!!!"

More than 70% of all communication is nonverbal. My friend Tim always flashed his 1000-megawatt smile, which of course, was a magnet. One of the most universal and clear nonverbal communications humans display is the smile. A smile says you're approachable and friendly. It invites engagement.

At an early age kids learn to read nonverbal communication—especially from their parents. Even when you think you're not responding, you're responding. Mine used to ask each other, "Does he have a mad face?" I can't say I smile all the time in my house, but I'm certainly aware of how my family takes cues from me. I'm acutely aware of the environment I co-create when I'm grumpy.

When you smile, you create a pleasant environment, another thing I learned from Tim. I also discovered that my intense nature has resulted in scores of people thinking I'm unapproachable or grumpy. We're still working on this, by the way. As I think back on the lessons I've learned from Tim, I'd have to say that adaptability is one of the greater ones. My frat or bruz as we used to say, were not conservative. They drank heavily, frequented the gentlemen's clubs, and rarely attended church. They'd often turn to one another and ask, "What's doing down tonight? The strip club." To which Tim would respond, "I'm down for whatever ya'll wanna do. You know me. I can go from 0 to 100 in a second," he'd laugh. He could go from drinking Hawaiian Punch after the Bible study with me to drinking shots of Petron at the strip club with the fellas.

He was the life of the party, always. Now, I'm not saying you need to go to strip clubs if that's not your thing, but we could all learn a valuable lesson from Tim. Being adaptable means being able to hang in any crowd. To have the ability to make people feel at ease around you is a precious gift, and Tim was great at it, which made him a highly effective leader, and I'm sure it also had something to do with him being made partner in a multi-million-dollar consulting firm that works with the likes of Kellogg's, Nestle, and other multi-billion-dollar food company icons.

Habit #6: Be Enthusiastic

One of my favorite shows of all time is *Seinfeld*. In this particular episode Jerry was talking to George, and they were trying to figure out if a girl liked George. One of the questions they asked to determine if she was in fact interested was, "When you answer the phone, does she greet you with an enthusiastic hello?"

George then explains that if he doesn't get an enthusiastic hello, he hangs up the phone because he's too intimidated to continue the conversation or ask for the date. He makes his biggest decision on a small detail. A very big, small detail.

If the girl's enthusiastic, it means she wants to hear from him and perhaps will enjoy seeing him. If, on the other hand, she doesn't show any enthusiasm, his belief is that asking for a date is a supremely bad idea.

What about you? When a person calls you or knocks on the door to your office, do you give them an enthusiastic hello? Or do you grumble or not respond at all?

Tim was a master at making people believe they had his undivided attention. If we were at dinner and someone stopped Tim, he'd get genuinely excited about talking to them. He'd give them a quick nickname and just like clock-work remember a tiny detail about them. "Hey, man, how was California?" or "I saw your dad the other day. He's looking great."

He just knows how to make people feel like they're the center of the universe, which in turn creates an incredible environment for work or play. His magnetism was a source of his influence. Leaders have a unique ability to walk into a room and make that room their playground. Not through manipulation or fake chitchat but rather by touching everyone in the room with a word, a glance, or a handshake.

Some executives pride themselves on being grumpy. They think it makes them more powerful. It may actually create the illusion of power for a while, but ultimately if this is your modus operandi, you won't lead for long. Not in today's business environment.

At the same time, the goal here is not to be the cheesy car salesperson either. I'm not talking about shooting people thumbs up or knocking them over the head with jargon and slick quotes or sayings. As much as the term's overused today, authenticity is what people respond to. Especially if that authenticity feels good.

One Final Thought on Enthusiasm

If I asked you to create a top 10 list of the most energetic people you've seen, who would make that list? You'd probably include a few sports coaches. You'd likely include a few fitness gurus. You'd probably talk about the late Billy Mays, who was the host of some of the biggest selling products via infomercials. We're all galvanized by energy. We're magnetized by it. It's infectious, which makes it highly influential.

HABIT # 7: EMPATHIZE

As I mentioned at the beginning of the book, back in 2004, I was in one of the deepest financial holes of my life.

I was close to $100,000 in the hole from my Expo business and another $20,000 with my real estate company. Ya'll, I was so broke I could barely pay attention.

I didn't see any way out and I was starting to feel desperate. Adding fuel to the fire was the fact that I had an eight-month-old baby daughter and wife at home. I don't have to tell you how stressful my life was back then. I had never been that far in debt, so I didn't have any experiences to draw from. I needed to be able to keep a roof over my family's head, and I needed to prove to myself that I wasn't a loser.

The market was down. The Expo was limping along, and the stress continued to mount. Every day there was something new. Bill collectors called and sent a barrage of letters to me. They harassed me, asking me to pay insane amounts of money I simply didn't have. They were relentless. The more they called, the more depressing the whole situation became.

Can you imagine not answering your phone because the person on the other end was going to remind you that you were in a dark hole? They'd call in the mornings. They'd call at night and on the weekends. They even started trying to contact people who knew me! It got so bad I even thought about changing my phone number.

In order to keep my head above water, I had to swallow my pride and ask Tim for a loan. I honestly never wanted that day to come but it had. My family needed me and there was no room for ego.

"Tim, man, I need to ask you a favor," I said.

I'm sure he already knew what was coming, but in true Tim fashion, he just listened.

"I'm in a bad place financially and I need to borrow some money." Even in his silence you could hear Tim's concern. I explained my situation, offered no excuses, and asked for his help.

There were a few seconds of silence before Tim finally spoke up. "Man, you know I would if I could, but we're in the middle of some major transitions in my company ... and I ... I just can't."

I understood and I could hear the disappointment in his voice. That's just the kind of cat Tim is. In fact, he's such a good brother that he offered to do a cash advance on his credit card to help me out. He knew I would not have asked unless I was in dire straits.

I told him I didn't want him to go into debt trying to help me out, so I declined his offer. But ya know what? I never forgot that moment in our friendship. It showed me even more who Tim was as a man. Had the shoe been on the other foot, honestly, my response would have probably been a bit different.

I certainly would have been concerned, but my tendency to be analytical, and maybe even a little judgmental, would have come out in the conversation. If I had the money I would have loaned it to him. However, the first thing I would have probably done is ask him a litany of questions. What happened? Did you have a budget? What was the backup plan? And, of course, the granddaddy of them all, "When you paying me back?"

Now, as you read those questions, some of you are squirming, but I'm just being honest. I would have wondered how a "smart" person could get themselves into such a pickle. How could a successful person be in such a bind? My natural tendencies are left brain. Give me tons of facts, figures, and details. His natural tendencies are right brain, emotional and concerned with how the other person must be feeling.

As much as you may be wired to think that left brain people lead better, the opposite is actually true. You need people who genuinely care about people to be in leadership positions. People will follow those they feel have a real concern for them and their well-being much faster than they will someone who wears data on their sleeves. I'm not saying numbers are insignificant. I'm saying I agree with Suze Orman, personal finance titan and host of CNBC's long-running syndicated money show, when she closes her weekly show with this mantra: People first, *then* money.

So, get out of yourself. The numbers are important yes, but as the old saying goes: When we're at the end of our lives, no one says things like, "Can you tell me if the stock market's up or down today?" Lead from the heart. Be empathetic and watch the fruit that will abound to your leadership account.

Habit #8: Listen

Influence is not about being the one with the most to say. When we're talking, we're not learning. So there's no other way to say this. If you want to be influential, shut up and listen up. Most people don't listen. Especially most high Choleric-oriented leaders. They tend to think the only person who has something relevant to say is them. They think they're the only one that's interesting or fascinating.

I want you to walk into a crowded room and see how much you can learn about everyone there. Watch how much insight and information you can get when you're genuinely interested in what other people have to say. People love talking about themselves, and they love people who will listen to even the seemingly mundane morsels of their lives. This is perhaps the greatest skill you can develop on the road to having more influence. Shut up and listen up.

When you feel yourself getting ready to turn the conversation back to you, don't. When you feel the urge to say, "Well, what I would do is ...," don't. When that burning desire to be the center of the world creeps up on you, squash it. Just silence it. And then, do what every influential leader in the world does all day, every day: Shut up and listen up.

Sometimes the skill of shutting up and listening up won't just improve relationships and give you greater influence. Sometimes your moments of brilliance come when you're not blabbering on at the mouth.

Take Kaile Warren, the founder of RENT-A-HUSBAND.

Kaile ran a small construction company. One day an accident forced him to shut it down, and soon he found himself drowning in debt at almost 40 years old. He was destitute and homeless. But it was in the midst of his despair that a great idea came to him. It was in a moment of "shut up and listen up" that he came up with the idea that saved his life and made him a global phenomenon.

With no money, no plan, and no hope, he looked around the beaten-up warehouse where he was sleeping and saw all the work that needed to be done to it. That's when the idea hit him.

So he went to a divorced women's shelter with a flyer that said simply: Need A Husband? Rent Me. He started asking women what they needed done. What kinds of things would they have a husband do if they had one? Instead of going into the shelter and telling them about his genius idea, he did what? Yep, he closed his mouth and listened.

He got over 50 calls and shortly thereafter launched RAH, which is now franchised all over the country. This guy went from homeless and hurting to becoming a national corre- spondent on CBS, a published author, and the leader of a growing company. He closed his mouth ... and listened. As a result he was able to uncover his market's needs and wants. He was able to solve their problems. Not surprisingly, he became extremely influential in the personal services space, which continues to help him grow his brand and bottom line.

Having the wisdom to know when to talk and when to shut up is an art lost on many people. Take ABC's hit show *Shark Tank.*

Entrepreneurs walk into a room where five self-made millionaires and billionaires are waiting to hear the latest and greatest entrepreneurial ideas. They've had folks pitch baked goods, jewelry, fitness equipment, and personal development products. It's the playground for the American dream.

Each week entrepreneurs take their chances at impressing the sharks and landing a deal. You can imagine the pressure they must feel as they stand before some of the richest folks in America and try to get them to invest in their company. It's a laboratory of deal-making, for sure. But it's also a lesson in knowing when to shut up and listen. Many of the entrepreneurs are terrible salespeople. They're not supposed to be great at selling necessarily. Their job is to show the sharks why they should invest in their companies.

As the stakes get higher for the entrepreneurs, their vulnerabilities surface. Invariably they slip into diarrhea of the mouth. They talk over the sharks. Forget their data. Sweat profusely, and basically try to talk their way into an investment. They don't know when to shut up.

Sometimes a shark will object to something the inventor or entrepreneur has said, which sends him or her into an auctioneer-style response where listening goes out the window. It's entertaining, but unfortunately it's also what kills a lot of deals in the Shark Tank.

As a leader your job is to know when it's advantageous to talk ... and when your best bet is to listen.

Habit #9: Question the Question (QTQ)

In addition to knowing when to speak and be quiet, great leaders and salespeople know that the key to closing isn't in monopolizing the conversation; it's in the quality of the questions asked during the sales process. True rainmakers take it a step further and they question the question. Let me explain.

Let's say you're doing a performance evaluation with one of your employees, and you want to get their take on why orange sneakers are outselling neon green ones. The employee you're talking to is a big college basketball fan.

You might say: Have you noticed that the orange sneakers have flatlined in the last few sales cycles?

Employee: Yep. I saw that in the report.

Leader: Why do you think that is?

Employee: I think it has something to do with all the top teams wearing highlighter green or accenting their uniforms with that color this March Madness.

Leader: That's interesting. So you think people are trying to align with the tournament or their favorite teams or players?

Employee: I do. I mean, have you seen Oregon's away uniforms?

Leader: No, I haven't. What are they like?

Now, the employee starts to describe the uniform, or he pulls out a computer to show you this new phenomenon around color in college sports. You've opened up a new level of communication with an employee that perhaps you knew very little about.

You started with a business question that allowed that team member to shine and educate you. But it goes even deeper. There's a new level of respect and rapport between the two of you that you can build on. And guess what? Your influence has grown because you not only questioned the question, but you also shut up and listened.

Before I learned the QTQ model, I always found a way to bring the conversation back to me. If someone returned from a trip to Canada, I'd say, "So, how was the trip?" They'd answer, "It was great, a little cold, but fun."

I'd then say, "Yeah, I went there two summers ago and we had a blast. We ...."

Today I question the question. "Was this your first time in Canada?" and "What was the weather like?" and "What was your favorite part of the trip?" When they share their world with you, they feel as though you understand them, thus they are more likely to allow you to lead them.

HABIT #10: BE OPTIMISTIC

In 2008, President Barack Obama made history by becoming the first African American to be elected to the White House. While he was very well educated, was on the forefront of using social media as part of a campaign, and by all accounts ran one of the most well-organized campaigns in election history, many credit his victory to this one word: optimism.

His campaign was one of hope and change. Or you could say optimism and opportunity. Many on the Republican side say he was unqualified for the job. They said he was inexperienced. The funny thing is many on the Democratic side said the same thing: too inexperienced.

Here you have a then-freshman senator that served one term in his state senate and who had no foreign relations credentials, yet he was elected in a landslide victory. For some, the jury's still out on his credentials, but regardless of whom you voted for in either of the elections, you can't deny that optimism is infectious. Obama infected the nation with his optimism.

The vast majority of those polled said his campaign was more positive and optimistic, which made his favorability numbers go through the roof. Even those who disagreed with his politics agreed he was likeable. No one wants to follow a negative leader. Obama never said, "I'm the best guy for the job." Instead he said, "I want to lead you to a better America."

We've all heard the saying from Zig Ziglar and other great motivational speakers, "Attitude, not Aptitude determines your Altitude." But your attitude also determines whether or not you are optimistic or pessimistic. Your attitude determines how you approach a situation and how you perceive people.

As with most things, your attitude evolves or develops over time. It isn't a disposition you are born with. This also means that if you have a negative attitude today, it's not a life sentence unless you choose to be that way.

There are three distinct phases of an attitude that you must understand if you're serious about becoming a magnetic leader: **thought, imagination,** then **manifestation** or **stronghold.**

THOUGHTS PACK POWER

Unless you're highly dysfunctional, you don't just wake up one day and have a negative attitude about someone or something. The seed of your negativity is a thought. Let's say you're an employer. You have an employee that always has a runny nose and is constantly in need of tissue. Around the same time you're noticing the guy in constant need of tissues, another good friend of yours reveals he (your friend—not the tissue guy) once had a cocaine addiction.

As a result of his addiction, your friend says, he not only cost the company several major deals, but he also stole thousands of dollars to support his habit.

Suddenly, guess what you're thinking? Maybe the guy with the runny nose is a cokehead. Maybe he's lying when he says it's allergies. Maybe he's stealing money from you. Maybe he's going to bring his addiction to work. Maybe ...

In the words of the world's leading authority on Kingdom Theology, Dr. Dana Carson, "Faith comes by hearing, and fear by thinking." You can't allow your thoughts to go unchecked. We're naturally self-protective, so your mind will always find ways to protect you from a potential problem, whether it truly exists or not.

Pretty soon, one thought has turned into 100 thoughts (an imagination)—none of which are based on any proof and all of which result from a tiny seed planted by the initial thought.

What happens in this phase is that you begin to think about the thought a bit too long. Then you begin to create even more "what ifs." What if one day this person steals all of our company's money? What if they cost me a couple of my big accounts? If I switched them to a different position where they are less prominent, perhaps they would pose less of a risk. None of the "what ifs" are facts, but that doesn't matter; they start to become a reality in your mind. As a result you begin to act and behave differently toward that person and then it graduates to the final phase of manifestation.

In this phase, your thoughts, beliefs, and actions have manifested. You become increasingly frustrated with the person, so what do you do? You fire them. Or the person starts to become rebellious and belligerent toward you and the company because they can sense the friction.

The resulting manifestation causes him to leave the company. Or they decide to stay with the company, but there's continual strain on the relationship because you have what I call a stronghold, a negative disposition or belief about someone or something that hinders the way in which you perceive and interact with a person.

These phases are evident in personal relationships as well. Take this fictional couple, Jack and Jill.

Jack and Jill have been married for a few years. Things have been pretty smooth sailing since their wedding. Jack comes home one night and casually mentions he's got a new boss. A woman. He doesn't say a whole lot about her except that she's from Chicago.

A few weeks later Jill attends a company function with Jack and meets his new boss, Madison Lacy. Not only is she vivacious, she's drop-dead gorgeous, something Jack never mentioned before.

A few weeks after the company event, Jack buys a new suit and decides to wear it one morning. He spends a few extra minutes in front of the mirror and puts on an extra spritz of cologne because he knows he's looking good.

On this particular morning Jill's running late. So she kisses Jack quickly and walks out the door. When she gets about a mile away from the house, she has a thought. Jack sure is looking dapper today. He never spends that much time on his wardrobe. And was he wearing cologne? What's with all the attention to personal grooming all of a sudden? What's going on?

Jill's starting to create a scenario in her mind based on what she believes are clues. As she drives down the highway to work, she starts to think back to the week Jack mentioned his new boss. She wonders why he never told her his boss was so attractive or dynamic. She wonders if he failed to mention those things because he's attracted to his boss. Or worse, he's got a crush on her. Or even worse, they're having an affair! Within a matter of minutes, guess what Jill's contemplating doing? Calling Jack and accusing him of having an affair, she is having an imagination!

Now, let's back this scene up and take it from Jack's perspective.

Jill's in a hurry, so she plants a quick kiss on Jack's cheek as she grabs her laptop and heads out the door.

Jack's left standing there, looking dapper. He has a quick thought. *Doesn't she see how good I look? She doesn't appreciate me. She takes me for granted.* His thoughts continue. *I notice she's been real distracted lately. I told her I had a big presentation today and not one word of encouragement.*

Now Jack's mood's changed. He's turned his attention away from his presentation and good looks to what could possibly be making Jill so unavailable and inattentive. So off he goes to the office. On his drive his thoughts start to spiral out of control. When he walks into his office, the cute new receptionist compliments him on his new suit and then asks about his cologne. "Is that tie new?" she asks. Jack feels even more unappreciated by his wife.

He begins to imagine how great it would be if he were single again—how much he'd be appreciated and how great it would be. He creates in his mind a fantasy land where all women recognize and appreciate him. But it doesn't stop there. In this fantasy land he gathers all the facts or negative things that Jill has ever done. By the time he reaches his desk, he's actually mad at Jill. So mad that he thinks about doing what? Yep, calling her to give her a piece of his mind.

Jack and Jill are both operating in their own worlds.

You see where I'm going with this? As I'm creating this picture, I'm actually laughing. As funny as this fictional scenario is, it's also played out in many marriages every single day. I've certainly had situations like this with my wife, where I was thinking one thing, and she was thinking another.

Imagine what happened when Jack and Jill got home later that night with the demands of their careers weighing heavily on their shoulders. They've had eight to ten hours to replay their perceptions out in their minds while they've been away from the other.

After a wonderful day in fantasy land, Jack finally comes home expecting to play out his fantasies. Jill's had time to do the same thing. When Jack walks into the house, instead of a warm greeting, he gets, "You're a little late, aren't you?"

Jack, who's convinced Jill's the wicked witch of the west, replies, "Didn't think it would matter."

From there the argument mounts. And for the next three hours this couple slings accusation after accusation at each other. All because of a single thought. Over time and without proper communication, a stronghold develops. He feeds the thought that she's unappreciative. She feeds the thought that because he didn't tell her how attractive his boss is, he must be hiding something else. All from one tiny thought.

Can thoughts be controlled? To some degree, yes. In Jack and Jill's case, it wasn't as much a matter of controlling their thoughts as it was of "checking in" as soon as the thoughts went to an unproductive and potentially destructive place.

When you get a thought in your mind, ask yourself, "Is this thought going to help me fulfill my ultimate purpose or goal?" If the answer is yes, feel free to think on it as long as you want. However, if the answer is no, cast the thought out of your mind and don't allow it to settle. Sometimes we're so afraid to admit the fears in our thoughts that we don't get a reality check from the person we're in a relationship with. Sometimes it's so difficult for us to simply turn to the people we love and say, "I had a crazy thought today."

By doing a quick check-in sometimes you can banish the thoughts that might lead to manifestation and escalation.

Did Jack and Jill fall down the hill?

Productive communication is the key and foundation of any healthy relationship. What is a marriage if the husband

and wife don't talk? Not much of a marriage at all. You have to learn how to communicate in a manner where the other person hears and feels heard.

Effective communication isn't about one person doing all of the talking and everyone else listening. It's about shared communication that moves us closer to our goal. In a marriage it's about doing what's best for the union. In business, it's about doing what moves the team forward, not one individual.

We can look at many instances where effective communication has resulted in positive results. While there's a great deal of furor surrounding what are considered "mega churches," no one can deny these churches are led by very charismatic ministers who have become great orators.

One of the most well-known mega churches is The Potter's House, led by Bishop T. D. Jakes. Walk into a Jakes service and you'll know exactly what I mean by communicating so that people hear and feel heard.

Jakes has become a legendary storyteller. He weaves a tale in a way that his parishioners not only understand but also enjoy. The more they enjoy the service, the more they are influenced by Jakes's teachings.

But communication and influence aren't just about talking.

Mother Teresa is a prime example of communication through her work. Influence through actions. Through her tireless commitment to serve, Mother Teresa changed the world. She influenced millions to elevate their generosity. She exemplified what it means to serve without expectation. She didn't stand at a podium and preach. She didn't blast out videos on YouTube and ask people to give money. She didn't take out a full page ad in The New York Times. She simply went about the business of serving. And on that one act alone, she influenced a nation.

The Art of Influence

As a motivational speaker, one of the biggest challenges I face when speaking to crowds of thousands of people or conducting extended leadership training—sometimes for hours—is to keep the audience engaged. That's when painting a picture comes in handy.

When a person speaks in images, individuals get mentally engaged. In 2003 I relocated to the Houston area and bought my second house. Upon finding the house, I did an inspection and found that the A/C wasn't working properly. I quickly requested that the seller fix the unit. A few days before closing, I asked, "Did you fix the air conditioning?" The seller was a great salesman and enthusiastically responded, "Oh yeah, it's fixed. I checked it the other day and it's like an icebox in there."

Growing up in the country, I frequently heard the term "icebox" to refer to a freezer or a refrigerator. So when he used the analogy of the icebox, I pictured the deep freezer we used to have at our house and remembered how cold it would get. It became a reality, in my mind.

Unfortunately, I didn't check to see if it had in fact been fixed, and after closing on the property, to my disappointment it was not "like an icebox in there." The guy had painted such a vivid picture that I believed him. He'd influenced me to take his words as gold.

Speaking in pictures is very influential. As the leader of a sales organization, you might launch a sales contest saying, "If you follow these steps, you'll be like a kingpin with big stacks of hundreds dollar bills on your desk." That's a vivid picture that would motivate most salespeople.

> If you run a nonprofit and you're trying to encourage your team to get more coat donations for the winter, try saying, "Imagine a five-year-old kid in a rundown apartment with no heat." Or you could go with a more positive slant and say, "Picture the smiles on the faces of hundreds of children as they receive their new winter coats."

LET QUALITY BE YOUR MEASURE

When I joined my fraternity, we had a saying, "Let quality be your measure." This simple saying guided us to represent our fraternity with pride. It meant do your best and don't measure yourself against others. Don't even measure yourself against the standard. Measure yourself against quality or excellence.

As the father of an eight-year-old who tends to be too much like her daddy, this can be a challenge. When I was younger, I used to rush through my schoolwork. If I had to write 10 sentences in 20 minutes, my goal was to be the first to finish. I was a pretty sharp kid, so I typically got high B's and most times A's; however, my work was not quality. It was not excellent. It was not the best it could be.

My daughter's following in my footsteps unfortunately. Recently, I was notified that she made two D's, one in math and the other in English. When I asked the teachers what the problem was, they both said the same thing. She doesn't take her time. She rushes through her work, and it's sloppy.

Her O's look like U's because she doesn't take the time to close them on top, and her 3's look like 2's. It's just a sloppy mess. Many of her answers were actually right, yet because it was not quality, it was illegible.

While I applaud my daughter for wanting to excel, my challenge is now to influence her work habits so that she doesn't sacrifice quality to be first. Because ultimately, if your work's not quality, you won't win. Not in the long haul.

So after getting the news about her recent grades, I had a little talk with her.

"I talked to your teachers today about your grades. They had some really good things to say about you."

Notice what I just did. I led with the positive. She could hardly believe what she was hearing. She fully expected me to lead with, "What's up with the D's?" Instead, I led with the positive.

"They did?" she said, surprised.

"Yeah, they think you're doing a great job," I said, trying not to laugh at how shocked she was. "How do you think you're doing?"

"Well ... I got a D," she said hesitantly. "Did they tell you that?"

I nodded yes. "Why do you think you got a D?"

She answered quickly, "I rush through my work."

I smiled and nodded. "Yep, Daddy used to do the same thing."

She giggled. "You did?"

"Yep. Why do you think you rush?"

She thought for a second. "Cuz I wanna get it done fast and be first."

"Why do you wanna be first?"

She thought a little harder. I could see her wheels turning. "Wellllll, because it's fun to be first."

I could tell she was sincere. She wasn't *trying* to get D's; she wanted the *rewards* of being first. But what my daughter didn't understand yet is the concept of quality.

"Listen, Daddy likes that you want to be first, but can I ask you a question? If you turn your paper in and half of your answers are incorrect, and a classmate walks up right after you and turns in her assignment but all of hers are correct, who do you think is really first?"

She understood. "Hers."

"Why?" I asked.

"Because if I made mistakes, then I have to go back and correct them, and turn them in again."

Bingo.

THE APPLE WAY

Few leaders have been under as much scrutiny as Apple's Steve Jobs.

I saw a special on Apple computers once where they discussed Jobs's relentless pursuit of excellence. One former executive talked about when they launched one of their computers, the start-up time was approximately 45 seconds, which was only a few seconds faster than the competition. He was proud of his accomplishment and was eager to present it to Steve.

It was reported that Jobs's response was typical of how he was known to respond in these situations, "Is that the absolute best you can do?" This particular executive was dismayed, but he went back to the lab shortly thereafter and miraculously cut another seven to eight seconds off the start-up time.

Former Pepsi executive John Sculley shared in several publications that Jobs would visit him in an attempt to woo him away from Pepsi to work for Apple. Among the things he told Jobs was that he thought Jobs should create the Apple Generation just as Sculley had created the Pepsi Generation. But what Sculley also said to Jobs that today's leaders should embrace is this: **We created ads depicting Pepsi as #1 because it was a psychological prerequisite to *becoming* #1.**

In other words, the seeds of influence must be planted systematically and methodically before they can take effect.

FINAL THOUGHTS

Becoming a super influential leader means first getting to know and understand your followers, then earning their respect, trust, and loyalty.

In his book *The Seven Spiritual Laws of Success*, Deepak Chopra says something that every leader needs to hear: In order to acquire anything in the physical universe, you have to relinquish your attachment to it.

Too many people are *trying* to be leaders. Too many people are trying to influence others. These efforts are generally coming from an ego-driven place. Now, all ego's not unproductive. In fact, our ego helps us out a lot. It tells us when danger's around the corner. It fuels our drive sometimes.

But when it comes to leadership, an overstimulated ego can be dangerous. Trying to get people to see you a certain way will almost always lead to them seeing you as a self-serving egomaniac. Not a good look for a leader.

To be an influential leader you simply need to embody the principles of leaders and influencers outlined for you in this book. Beating your chest and telling people to follow you will have the opposite effect for sure.

Approaching leadership as a privilege, as an honor and not as a right, positions you to become the leader people want to follow. That's the essence of the blueprint I've laid out for you in *Love Them and Lead Them.*

Be quick to listen and slow to talk. Help others achieve their deepest desires and wildest dreams, and when big decisions have to be made, when life throws your team or relationship a curve ball, or when the organization is ready to go to the next level, they'll turn to you, wait for your word, and gladly follow your lead.

PART III TAKEAWAYS

- You can't have influence without the respect of your followers.

- Influence is not about manipulation.

- Leaders influence through actions as well as words.

- Let quality be your measure.

- Influence is subtle yet powerful.

- Influence is the result of deliberate actions over time.

- Effective communication never assumes.

- Influence is emotional, not logical.

- Influence happens as a byproduct of learning to love, understand, lead, and honor the people you're privileged to lead.

- Law of Help: People feel significant when they're able to help someone else.

BONUS SECTION

Of all the things I have learned along my leadership journey, learning to understand different personality temperaments has yielded me the greatest return. Once you grasp an understanding of how these personalities work and how to effectively utilize them, you will be amazed at the results you can achieve with them. It is almost like you can read a person's mind.

Though I touched on it briefly earlier in the book, as a special bonus here are a few tips and techniques to help you understand each temperament and how to flip the automatic switches that make them more likely to respond favorably to you as a leader. I'll also show you how to quickly identify the personality type by a simple handshake.

SANGUINE

STRENGTHS:

The Sanguine is the most extroverted of all the personalities. They love to laugh and genuinely love people. Sanguines are gifted linguists and tend to dominate most conversations whether they have anything relevant to say or not. As you can imagine, they love the limelight and are typically very good salesman and public speakers.

Optimistic by nature, the Sanguine is typically upbeat. He or she easily forgets the past and has very little fear. It is not uncommon for the Sanguine to have several projects going on at once, and if one fails, he or she can easily transition to another, forgetting past failures.

WEAKNESSES:

Though the Sanguine is extremely popular and loved by most, at times this can come with a cost. As a result of their desire to please people, they can be weak willed, very undisciplined, and at times unreliable. Sanguines are very egotistical and notorious for being disorganized; they seldom plan ahead. Because of their ability to easily forget the past, they seldom learn from past mistakes.

Sanguines are best suited for sales and marketing positions. Leading a team can pose inherent challenges for Sanguines as their desire to be liked, coupled with their weak will, can cause them to cave to the whims of those they are supposed to lead; they also strive to avoid conflict.

How to Manage a Sanguine:

Always heed my 3 Step Connection plan. Sanguines are highly relational, so you must establish a connection with them before you get down to business. Put them in your customer service or sales positions to benefit from their people skills. When addressing an infraction with them, talk in terms of the people—what the team is doing. Remember their worst fear is social rejection; they would never want to be an outcast or social reject.

Sanguine Handshake:

The quickest way to identify a personality temperament is to shake his or her hand. A Sanguine is notorious for the extended handshake and loves the two-hand sandwich coupled with the shoulder tap. They are touchy-feely people; thus they get every bit of pleasure possible from a handshake.

CHOLERIC

Strengths:

Cholerics are highly aggressive, competitive, confident, and self-disciplined people who have an extreme desire to win. They typically never give up, which results in a high completion rate for their projects. Though they reach most of their decisions using their intuition, they are naturally left brain, black-and-white oriented individuals. They readily accept leadership, are good judges of people, and have forceful natures that tend to dominate groups. As a result of their self-confidence, they are typically very optimistic and not easily swayed by other people's opinions. Research also suggests that this is the rarest of all the personality temperaments.

Weakness:

A negative by-product of the Choleric's extreme self-confidence is that they tend to diminish the value of others. Though they get things accomplished, they hate details; they are big-picture, end-result oriented. They are highly insensitive and have little to no regard for other people's feelings; they also tend to be very judgmental. They often try to instill fear in and intimidate those who oppose their wishes; they are notorious for extreme outbursts of anger. A Choleric says what he or she thinks with no sensitivity at all for others' feelings, which can result in many hurt feelings and can cause others to draw the conclusion that he or she is a jerk.

How to Manage Choleric:

Always keep in mind the "S" and the "O" in my S.T.O.P. analysis. What is the Choleric's significance to the organization? Remember, these are the ones who can drive a project and get things done. They are extremely useful people. Also, look at the outcome. If the outcome of their value is positive, you may have to look the other way and endure their antisocial ways as long it is not a detriment to the team or the overall goal. Remember, their uncaring ways are natural to them. Most are completely oblivious to the fact that others can't stand them as they really don't care. They measure success by results, not relationships. Lastly, remember they are ego maniacs, so stroke their egos. Tell them how great they are and ask them how they came up with such a brilliant idea and if they could share their insights with the team.

CHOLERIC HANDSHAKE:

When you shake a Choleric's hand, brace yourself! They tend to be the ones with the crushing handshake as they attempt to show their dominance and power. They typically won't release pressure until you release first; for them, it's a competition. A sure test you can perform to see if you are dealing with a Choleric is, when shaking their hand, turn your hand counterclockwise so that your hand is on top and theirs is on the bottom. Their subconscious—and instant—reaction will be to turn back in the other direction. They can't stand you being on top; they must win at all costs.

MELANCHOLY

STRENGTHS:

Melancholies are highly self-disciplined and intelligent individuals who are sticklers for details. They can quickly analyze a project and point out potential problem areas. Because they are very adept at creative thinking, if a problem arises, it is not uncommon for them to invent a solution. Not prone to egotism, the Melancholy rarely seeks the limelight but can always be relied upon to complete the task at hand in the prescribed manner.

WEAKNESSES:

An unwanted side effect of the Melancholy's perfectionist mentality is that they can be extremely pessimistic and negative people. Their worst fear is being wrong; because of this, they can be slow at times. They will not move until they have all the details they need to ensure things are done "right." They are the opposite of the Choleric and will start a project with no details as their confidence makes them think they can figure it out. Melancholies are impossible to please and extremely critical of others as well as themselves, which can result in bouts of depression.

HOW TO MANAGE A MELANCHOLY:

Remember my Law of Respect and Law of Permission and understand that a Melancholy's greatest fear is being wrong. Instead of telling them what to do, which will inherently lead to a barrage of questions, ask them what they think. Give them the problem, and let them be involved in the creation of a solution. Remember, they are inventors; they can invent solutions and troubleshoot potential problems.

MELANCHOLY HANDSHAKE:

Remember the Melancholy is consumed with doing things right. Thus their handshake will be picture-perfect. They will ensure that they look you in the eyes, firmly grasp your hand, and pump up and down no more than three times for a duration of no more than five seconds. You will never be able to accuse them of shaking your hand the wrong way.

PHLEGMATIC

STRENGTHS:

Phlegmatics are extremely introverted individuals who are very loyal. They are tremendous team players and will never initiate conflict; they will always allow others to "win" in order to avoid potential friction. They are very thoughtful and will think things through before beginning; they don't like change. Phlegmatics are very dependable, good-natured, cheerful, and are natural-born diplomats. They always prefer compromise over altercation. Phlegmatics are the Choleric's best friend as they are the only ones that allow him to bulldoze his way around without a challenge. Research also suggests that this is also the most common temperament.

WEAKNESSES:

Phlegmatics tend to lack drive and ambition, which creates a negative by-product—slowness. In addition, as a result of their desire to avoid conflict, they tend to bottle up their emotions, resulting in major explosions when they do finally let go of those emotions. Most studies would suggest that these are the people who "go postal." They rarely initiate a project and are masters at creating excuses not to get involved. Phlegmatics are very thin-skinned and surprisingly stubborn, highly selfish individuals who are masters at disguising their true intentions.

HOW TO MANAGE A PHLEGMATIC:

With the understanding that a Phlegmatic is very important to your team, you must be patient. Also, remember my 3 Step Connection plan: they are relational and want to feel appreciated and valued. Talk to them using very encouraging and reassuring words that will make them feel comfortable expressing their feelings. With their natural skill for negotiation to avoid conflict, they are also well suited for customer service positions.

PHLEGMATIC HANDSHAKE:

The Phlegmatic handshake is the easiest to identify and is characterized by the limp hand. These are the ones who grab the tips of your fingers, blocking full palm-to-palm contact. It is a submissive move, and they need to warm up to you before they get too close.

FINAL NOTE ON TEMPERAMENTS

Remember no one is all one temperament or another; we are blends. For myself, I have found that while I am most certainly Choleric, my Choleric tendencies are more dominant when I am at home with my wife and children. However, in the corporate setting I have a number of Phlegmatic and Melancholy tendencies.

These tips are simply guides that can help you be more successful. Understanding temperaments is a powerful element to add to your leadership arsenal. It helps you understand the people you lead. It is what the Love Them and Lead Them leadership model is all about—people.

How to Get More Information from the Author

Other Books by Jerome Love

Get Up, Get Out & Get Something: How Contrapreneurship Can Help You Build a Booming Business!

Get Up, Get Out & Get a Degree: 3 Simple Steps to Ensure that You Graduate in 4 Years or Less!

Get Up, Get Out & Get a Diploma: 3 Strategies to Ensure that You Graduate with Your Class!

Becoming Your Own Boss (Action Guide)

Business Planning for Success (Action Guide)

All Books, Action Guides, and Audio Series are available at www.jeromelove.com.

Other Suggested Reading

How to Persuade People Who Don't Want to Be Persuaded, Joel Bauer & Mark Levy

Be the One, Jonathan Sprinkles

Incarnational Leadership, Dana Carson, PhD

The Ultimate Marketing Plan, Dan Kennedy

The Ultimate Sales Letter, Dan Kennedy

The 21 Irrefutable Laws of Leadership, John Maxwell

Primal Leadership, Daniel Goleman, Richard Boyatzis & Annie McKee

Start with Why, Simon Sinek

Why We Buy, Paco Underhill

Influence, Rober Cialdini

Why You Act the Way You Do, Tim LaHaye

Permission Marketing, Seth Godin

EPILOGUE

Congratulations! You did it.

I hope you enjoyed taking the Love Them and Lead Them Challenge with me. But hold on, it's not over yet. Go back and read it again. Then take what you've learned and start implementing it today. Take my laws and principles out for a test drive and watch how your relationships at home and work get remarkably better.

I've poured my heart and soul onto the pages of this book, revealing some pretty horrific character flaws and train wrecks I had to endure to get where I am today. I couldn't in good faith and conscience just share the highlights of my journey; I had to share the hard times as well because it's in those moments our true character's revealed.

I know I'm not defined by the mistakes I've made but by the subsequent and continual efforts I've made to become a better friend, husband, father, CEO, and leader. There's no question that the principles I've shared with you have transformed my life and businesses, and I'm 100 percent confident they'll do the same for you.

If you take nothing else away from this book, know this: Everything, and yes I mean everything, creates your own personal brand. And you brand will either attract or repel followers. Whether you smile or always have a mean face, whether you take an interest in others or not, whether you greet others or whether you don't, all of that goes into your brand. It is not just your ability to get results!

It's been my honor and pleasure to share these leadership lessons with you in the hope that you'll have the courage to face your own demons, shortcomings, and insecurities and step up to the leadership plate and knock it outta the park every chance you get.

Drop me a line in the next few months. I mean it. I want to hear about your struggles and successes. And if I can ever be of assistance to you or your organization, don't hesitate to contact me at jerome@jeromelove.com. Here's to a lifetime of loving them and leading them.

God Bless.

Jerome Love

ABOUT THE AUTHOR

JEROME LOVE

Jerome Love was voted **Entrepreneur of the Year** (NBMBAA), **Pinnacle Award Finalist** (HCCOC), **Multi-Million Dollar Top Producer** (Prudential Texas Realty), and is a favorite keynote speaker amongst both corporate and collegiate audiences.

Here's why: he's funny; His energetic style and vivid stories keep audiences on the edge of their seats as he candidly share practical steps to how anyone can achieve the prosperity and lifestyle they desire.

Throughout his 16 year career, as an entrepreneur and professional speaker Jerome has been consistently recognized as a well-respected and sought-after expert in sales and business development. The author of several books, his writings have been published nationally and are frequently quoted by industry experts. Jerome's keynote has been featured on major platforms such as the Los Angeles Mayors Economic Development Summit and he has shared the stage speaking at conferences with global icons such as Jeff Hoffman (Founder of Priceline.com), Susan L. Taylor (Publisher Emeritus, Essence Magazine), and Michael Delazzer (Founder of Redbox), just to name a few. Though his presentations range in topics, Jerome's true passion and the focus of his bestselling book, "Get Up, Get Out & Get Something", is helping people perform at their best and building highly profitable businesses.

His passions stems from the agony that he felt when he began his first business at the age of 19 with high hopes of prosperity, yet ended up in the hole more than $100,000, by the age of 25. However, Jerome's relentless determination wouldn't allow him to give up. Refusing to settle for life's second best, he decided to Get Up, Get Out & Get Something. In 2002, he founded the Texas Black Expo, Inc. which now produces the largest African American Tradeshow in Texas. He wrote his first book at age 30, and is the Broker of LHS Realty Group a leading real estate firm headquartered in Houston, TX, the nations 4th largest cities.

Upon writing his book, available at www.jeromelove.com, Love then launched his career as a professional speaking.

Speaking for corporations, associations, colleges, & universities Love transparently shares how he turned his repeated struggles into incredible success and uses interactive examples to prove how anyone (even the most apathetic individual) can dig deep within and to discover the *motive* that fuels their *motivation*.

Love's keynote is ideal for corporate luncheons, business galas, leadership events, staff and employee development, plus more! For booking and product information visit **www.jeromelove.com**.

He Did It AGAIN!

Jerome Love showed a packed audience of students at Danville Community College how to take ownership of their college experience and use their power to Get Up, Get Out & Get Something™, become self motivated, and **GRADUATE!**

Jerome Love,
the GUGOGS™ GUY,
Empowering People.
Changing Lives.

As Seen On

"WOW! Thank You! Thank You! Thank You! Those are are the words I keep hearing from those who attended your presentation. I've never scene a group of students more mesmerized and enthralled as I saw at this event. More than 400 students were absolutely captivated by your presentation. I've never scene anything like it. In one word it was AMAZING!" - **Linda Wilborne, Danville Community College (Danville, VA)**

Ideal For: Corporate Luncheons
• Opening Ceremonies • Welcome Week
• Awards Banquets • Sales Events
• Leadership Retreats • Entrepreneurial
Programs • Plus More!

You can be next! Find out the top reasons coordinators invite Jerome back again and again and how you can get a FREE talk for your group! ➜

Top 4 Reasons Why Event Coordinators Invite Jerome Back Again and Again!

1 His energetic style and vivid stories keep audiences on the edge of their seats. **This means you will always receive rave reviews, making you look like a genius!**

2 His Total Transformation package comes with $750 in free books! **These can be used for prizes, rewards for attendance, gifts, or whatever you choose!**

3 Jerome has a hassle-free guarantee. You don't have to worry about any unnecessary rider requirements – all he needs is a microphone and a bottled water! **This means, you don't have to deal with any additional or unnecessary charges, fees, or expenses!**

4 Jerome Love's **MORE** than money back guarantee. If for any reason you're not satisfied with his program, he'll give you your money back, and give you 50 FREE books for your trouble! **This means, you don't have to worry. There is NO risk!**

Jerome Love, The GUGOGS™ GUY,
Speaker / Author / Contrapreneur™

www.jeromelove.com

Check Out This AMAZING Success Story!

DCC
Danville Community College

Serving Danville * Halifax County * Pittsylvania County

1008 South Main Street * Danville, Virginia 24541-4004
434.797.2222 * TTY: 434.797.8542
Fax: 434.797.8541 * www.dcc.vccs.edu

Hi Jerome,

WOW!! And Thank You. Thank You. Thank You. Those are the words I keep hearing from those who attended your speaking event here at Danville Community College. The comments keep pouring in from people about how great you were. I have had emails and phone calls, thanking me for bringing you here and commenting on the difference you have made in their lives. I have had numerous calls from people who weren't able to attend and have talked to some who did and they want to know when you are coming back. Many have said they want to come back and hear you again. There was one high school principal in the audience who saw two of his students there with their mothers. He said he was so glad to see them because you were just what they needed (and they were on spring break but still attended). He said he definitely wants to collaborate with DCC when you come back and have you come to speak at this high school. One student who won third place in the competition told the newspaper reporter he had never dreamed it was possible for him to start a business but after hearing you, he knew he could and was seriously thinking about it. I spoke to the high school teachers and they all had stories of how their students talked about nothing else on the way back to school but your words to them. We had the students complete a brief survey rating the event 1-5 with 5 being excellent. Two students asked if they could rate you a 10. They said excellent was not good enough for you and what they heard you say. The raving compliments about you have been endless.

Jerome, thank you so much for giving us the opportunity to hear you. You will definitely be asked to come back. You mentioned the possibility of speaking, perhaps at our orientation in the early fall. I'm going to try to get this going. It was such a pleasure working with you. You have touched many lives here and made a difference to people you may never know, but, they know you. Thank you for all your hard work and all that you do. Have a great summer and I hope to be talking to and seeing you soon. You truly are a DYNAMIC speaker!

Linda Wilborne

Assistant Professor of Business Management
Danville Community College
1008 South Main St.
Danville, VA 24541-4004
Email lwilborne@dcc.vccs.edu
Tel. 434-797-8407
Fax 434-797-8488

An Equal Opportunity/Affirmative Action College * Member, Virginia Community College System

Could all these people be wrong?

Executive Leadership

"The principles that Love shares are a rare thing. He gives clear actionable steps for success as a leader. If you desire to know the real truth about leadership, the principles that Love shares are certain to get you there."
~ **Jeff Hoffman, Founding Team Member, Priceline.com**

"Love's story is amazing and I thoroughly enjoyed his energetic and engaging style."
~ **Susana Martinez, Governor, State of New Mexico**

Colleges & Universities

"The GUGOGS™ presentation is nothing short of AMAZING! It's a powerful presentation that not only taught powerful principles but kept the students' attention with its entertaining style. It was simply phenomenal!"
~ **Tim Putnam, Associate Director, North Iowa Area Community College John Pappajohn Entrepreneurial Center (Mason City, IA)**

"The GUGOGS™ presentation was one of the very best workshops and seminars I have attended. He utilizes his personal experiences to entertain his audience while making entrepreneurship plain and simple."
~ **Richard Leake, Professor of Economics & Management, Luther College (Decorah, IA)**

"Our students absolutely loved the GUGOGS™ business presentation. That's all they have been talking about. They found the principles in this lecture to be relevant, practical, and presented in an entertaining manner that really inspired them!"
~ **Susan G. Duffy, Ph. D., Assistant Professor, Simmons College School of Management (Boston, MA)**

Book your date within 30 days of purchase, and you'll get 50 FREE books for your group!

Enrollment Form

Organization:	_____	**Contact:**	_____
Your Name:	_____	**Email:**	_____
Address:	_____	**City:**	_____
State/Zip:	_____	**Phone:**	_____

Product Information

Please fill in quantity and tally total investment.
Most products qualify for _**continuing education & learning materials**_ budget and reimbursement.

Title	Type	Investment	Quantity	Total
Get Up, Get Out & Get Something: How Contraprenuership Can Help You Build a Booming Business	Book	$15		
Get Up, Get Out & Get Something Presentation	DVD	$30		
Get Up, Get Out & Get Your Diploma	Book	$15		
Love Them and Lead Them	Book	$20		
Becoming Your Own Boss"	Action Guide	$30		
How to Write a Compelling Business Plan	Action Guide	$30		
Total Investment				

Get Up to	50 – 100	10%	
50% Off	101 – 250	20%	1,000 +
Select Products with the	251 – 500	30%	50%
Following Price Breaks:	501 – 1,000	40%	

Enrollment Information. Please PRINT CLEARLY.

Payment Type:	MC / Visa / Discover / Invoice	**Cell Phone:**	_____
Name on Card:	_____	**CC#:**	_____
Exp. Date:	_____		_____
Invoice Contact Information:			_____

Make check payable to JeromeLove.com and mail to the address below:

Phone: 888-225-1918   Fax: 832-615-3065   Web: www.JeromeLove.com
12401 S Post Oak Suite 218 Houston, TX 77045